Compiled by Sun Bingshan

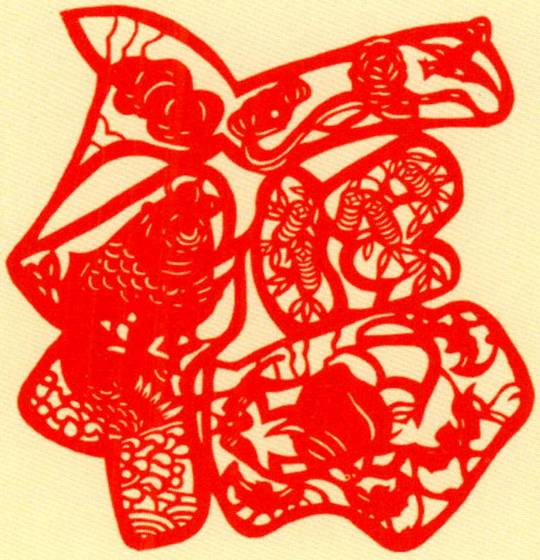

CHINESE PAPER-CUTS

CHINA INTERCONTINENTAL PRESS

图书在版编目（CIP）数据

中国剪纸：英文／孙秉山编著；严马，王国振译.—北京：五洲传播出版社，2008.1
（中国民间工艺品丛书）
ISBN 978-7-5085-1212-9

Ⅰ.中… Ⅱ.①孙…②严…③王… Ⅲ.剪纸－民间工艺－中国－英文
Ⅳ.J528.1

中国版本图书馆 CIP 数据核字（2007）第 171792 号

策　　划：荆孝敏
编　　者：孙秉山
翻　　译：严　马　王国振
特约编辑：吕　蕾
责任编辑：王　莉
装帧设计：缪　惟　林国霞

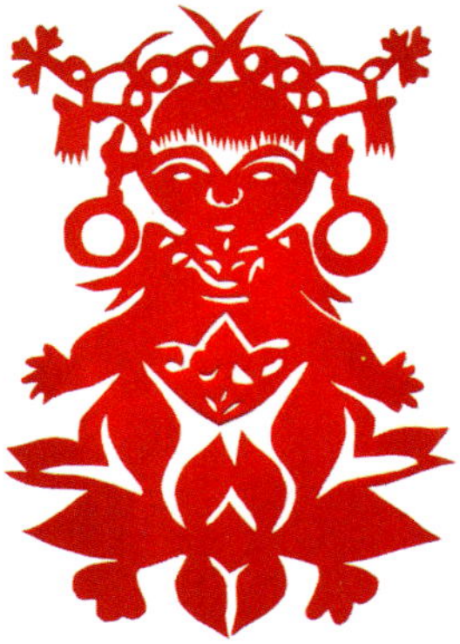

中国剪纸

出版发行：五洲传播出版社
社　　址：北京市海淀区莲花池东路北小马厂 6 号华天大厦
邮政编码：100038
电　　话：010-58891281
传　　真：010-58891281
制版单位：北京锦绣圣艺文化发展有限公司
印　　刷：北京朗翔印刷有限公司
开　　本：889x1194　1/24
印　　张：4.5
版　　次：2008 年 10 月第 2 版　2008 年 10 月第 1 次印刷
书　　号：ISBN 978-7-5085-1212-9
定　　价：68.00 元

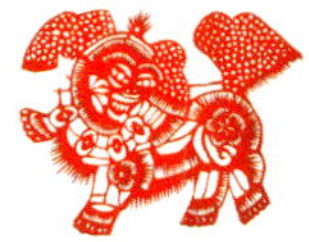

Preface

Chinese paper-cutting boasts a long history. As early as the period of the Emperor Wu Di of the Han Dynasty over 2,100 years ago, records show that someone made a paper-cut of the image of Li Furen, the late favourite concubine of Emperor Wu Di, so as to comfort him in his sorrow. During the Southern Dynasties (420-589) it became a custom to paste well-cut thin silk in the shape of a person on screens for festivals. In springtime, during the Tang Dynasty (618-907), people would cut coloured pieces of silk, paper or gold foil into various shapes such as swallows, flowers or butterflies, which were presented as gifts, pinned on the hair, hung on willow branches or pasted on screens. It added colour to the early spring.

Today this custom is carried on in most households, particularly during the Spring Festival, by hanging streamers on the door jambs and sticking paper cuts to the windows for decoration.

Even as a plastic art the paper-cut has its unique charm. It is extremely concise in its artistic form simply cutting some holes in different places on a piece of paper. The final image on the paper-cut comes into being from the contrast of the solid part and the empty part. This technique is one of the particularities of Chinese traditional artistic creation. This style originates from the Chinese traditional concept of the universe which is that "*Yin* and *Yang* (the two opposing principles in nature) created the world."

In this modern era there are various types of paper-cuts for different purposes and they may basically be divided into five categories. Except for several pieces in the book, all the other paper-cuts were collected from the rural areas some 20 years ago.

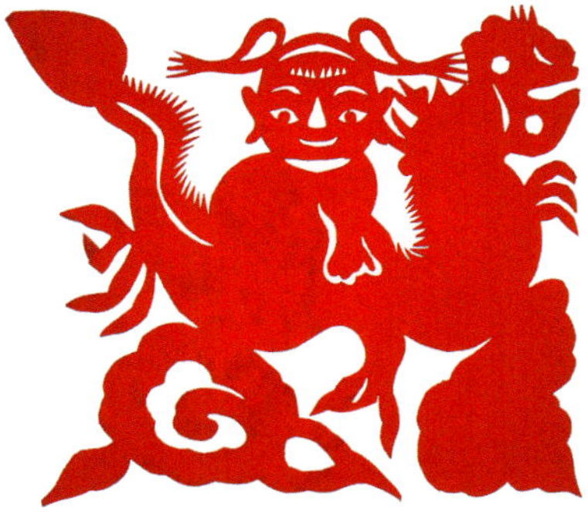

[CONTENTS]

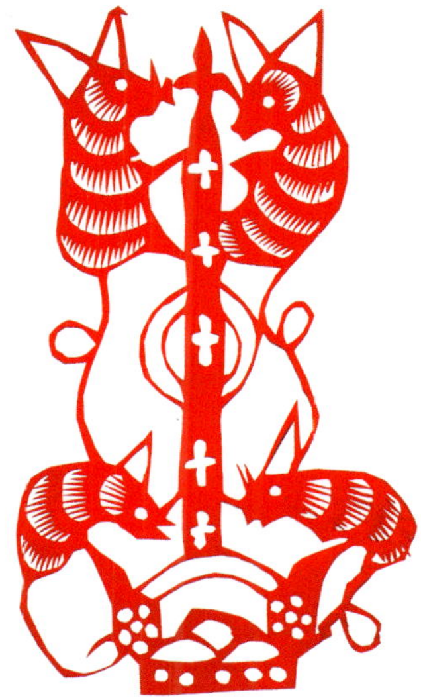

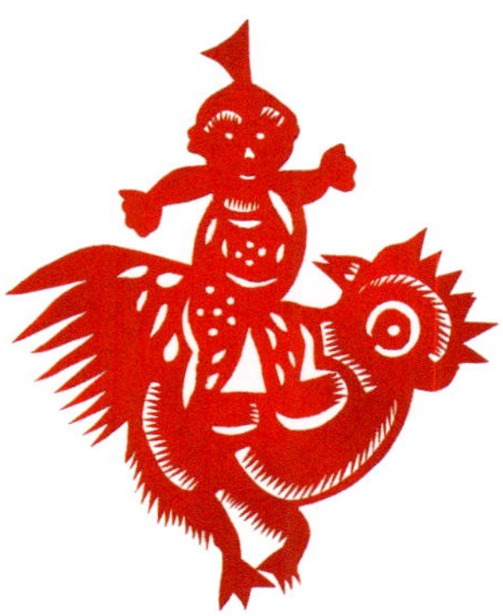

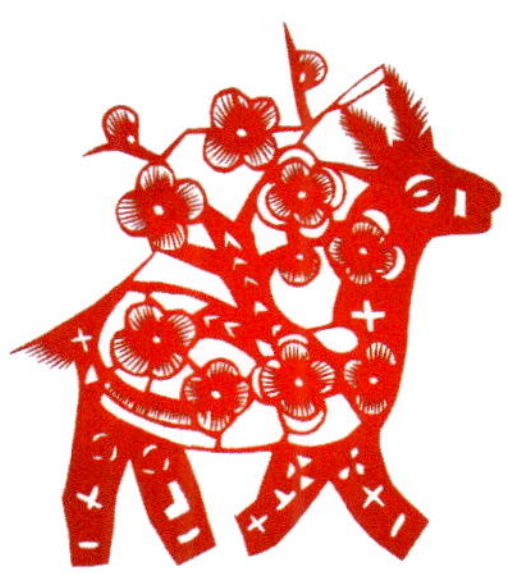

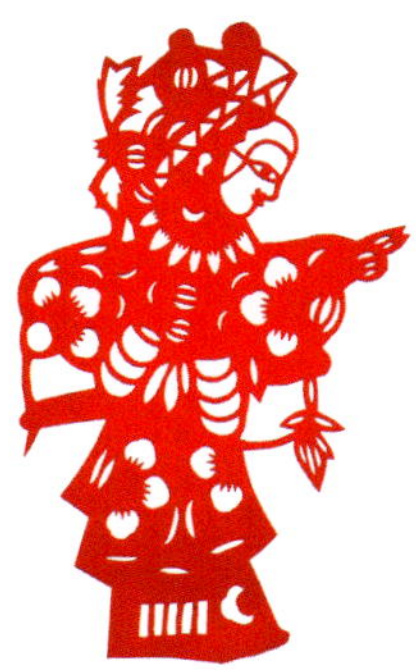

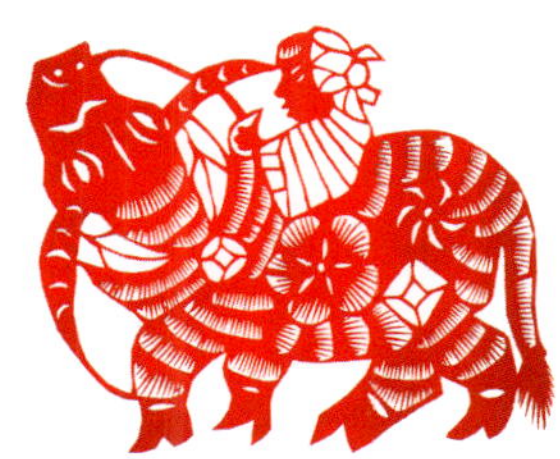

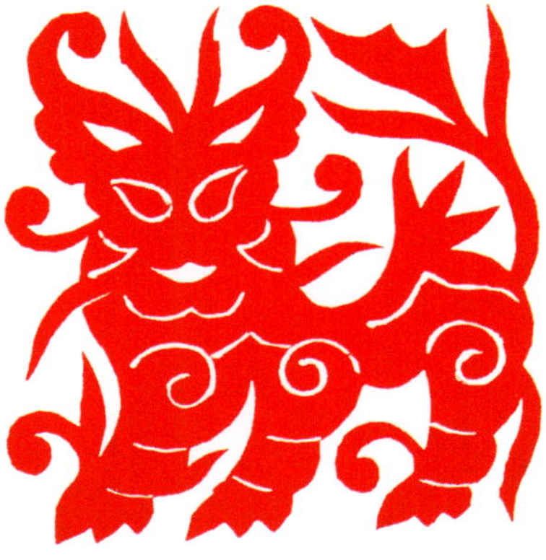

Category of Streamers

All the paper-cuts used in such activities as praying for blessings, offering sacrifices, eliminating disasters and diseases and exorcising evil spirits belong to this category. During the Spring Festival households in many areas in China like to paste colourful streamers on the doors of their courtyards, houses, rooms and even cabinets. This type of streamer is actually a symbol used for worshiping heaven, earth and ancestors so as to pray for blessings, avoid disasters and exorcise evil spirits.

There is an old tale which goes like this: after Jiang Ziya helped the King of Wu found the Western Zhou Dynasty (1100 BC-771 BC), he praised and deified the loyal officials and generals of both the Shang (1600 BC-1100 BC) and Western Zhou (1100 BC-771 BC) Dynasties who had died in the war of dynastic change. After he had finished his wife came to him and shouted at him,"How will you deify me?." He thought for a while and answered,"Poor deity because wherever you go you will bring poverty." "Your principal behaviour is to come back if you see poverty and dilapidation so as not to bring greater misfortune to the poor people there."

Therefore on festive days people paste streamers with many holes cut in them on the door so as to keep the "poor deity" away.

Here is another example. On the fifth day of the fifth lunar month, people paste paper-cuts in the shape of a "rooster" and a "mugwort-plaited tiger," which can vanquish the five poisonous creatures, on their doors and the "House-guarding Tiger" on the walls of the houses. This is a custom with a history of over 1,000 years.

More than 1,200 years ago, Du Fu, a great ancient Chinese poet,wrote "warm water washes my feet and paper-cuts evoke my spirit." This is testament to the long history of the Chinese people using paper-cuts to help them think of good things and forget evil.

This kind of paper-cut has a very short service life. That of the streamers pasted on the door-jamb during the Spring Festival and the "tiger" and the "rooster" pasted on the fifth day of the fifth lunar month is less than one month and that of the spirit-evoking streamers used for exorcising evils and getting rid of diseases is less than half an hour. Such papercuts are normally not preserved but are burned after the activity or during the course of the activity.

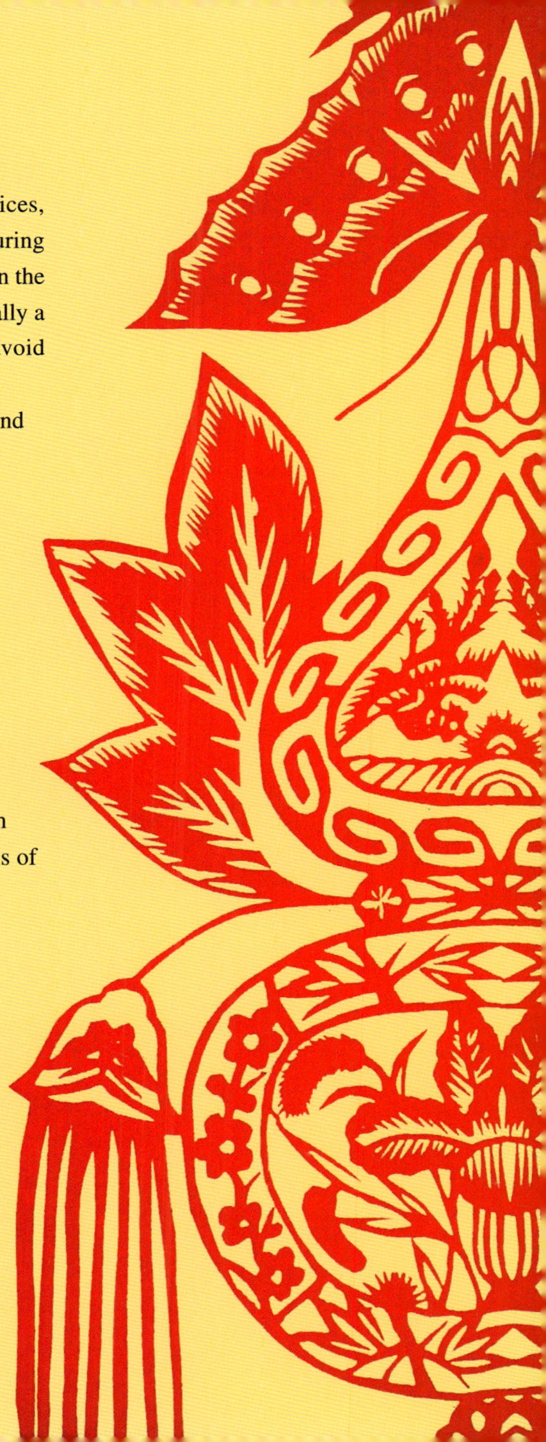

2

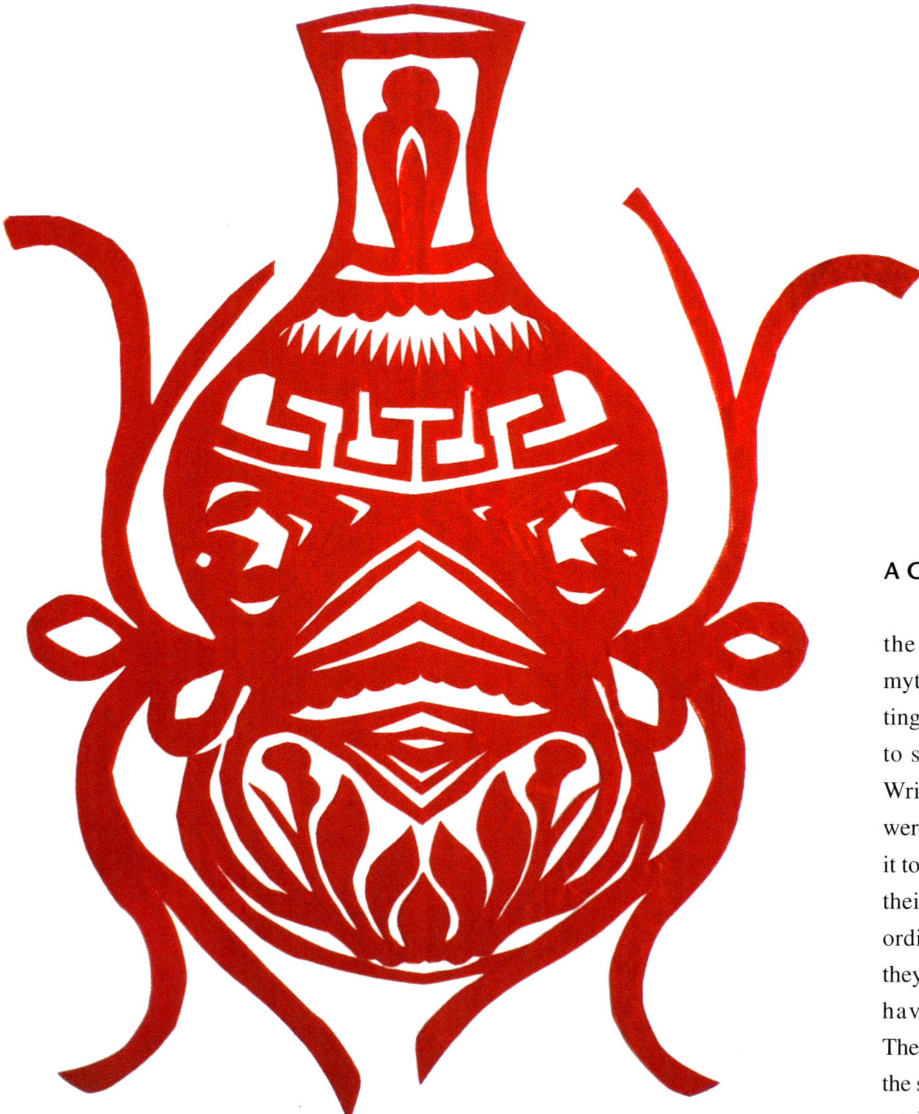

A Gourd

The Chinese seem to like the gourd. The immortals in myths loved it, not only for putting elixir in it, but also using it to subdue spirits and demons. Writers and scholars in society were fond of it and not only used it to hold wine, but also put it on their tables for inspiration. The ordinary people like it because they think of it as a treasure and having magical properties. Therefore, pasting a paper-cut in the shape of a gourd in the house could not only exorcise evil but also bring luck to the family.

Cutting off the Five Poisonous Creatures

The period around the fifth day of the fifth month is commonly referred to as "the evil days" because this is when poisonous insects breed and diseases can start as a result. Therefore, every family pastes paper-cut gourds on their door and walls to subdue the five poisonous creatures (referring to scorpions, snakes, centipedes, geckos and toads) and avoid plagues. A scissor shape is usually hidden in the gourd with the meaning of cutting off the five poisonous creatures.

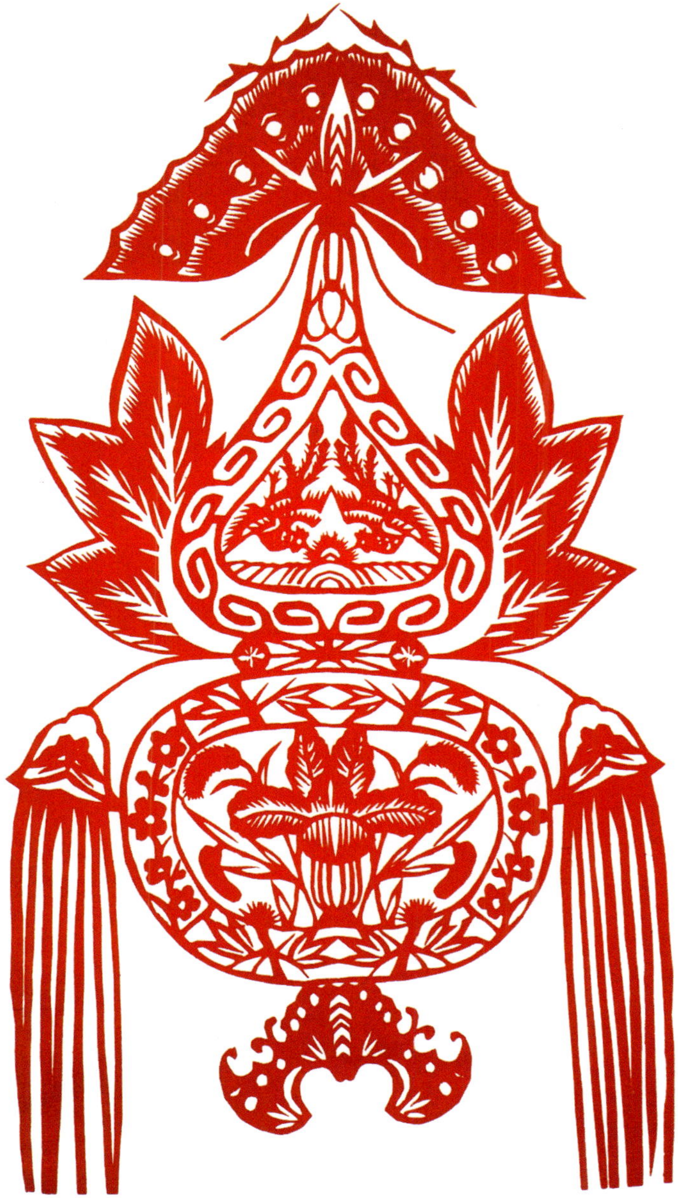

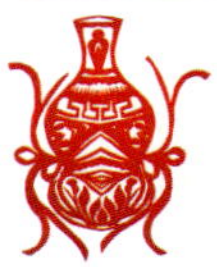

The Sky Sweeping Woman

During the heavy summer rains a farmer's wife may hang a paper-cut of the sky-sweeping woman in the courtyard and this is said to be able to prevent rain. It is said that the sky-sweeping woman is the ancestor Nuwa. In the picture she is clearing away the rain clouds in the sky with her right hand and sweeping water away on the earth with her left hand. She reputedly has the fearless spirit of being able to patch the sky, fight floods and relieve disasters.

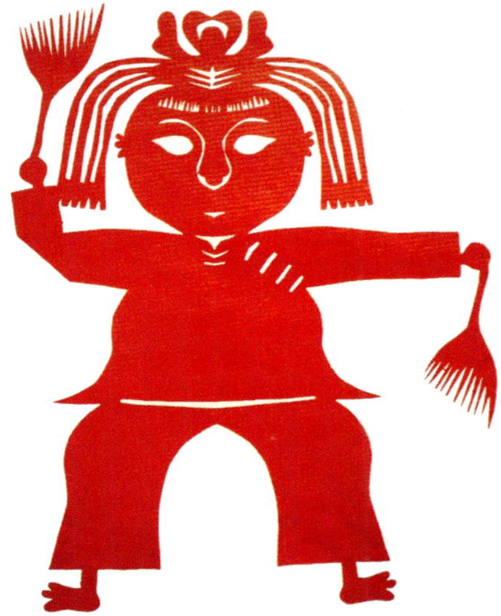

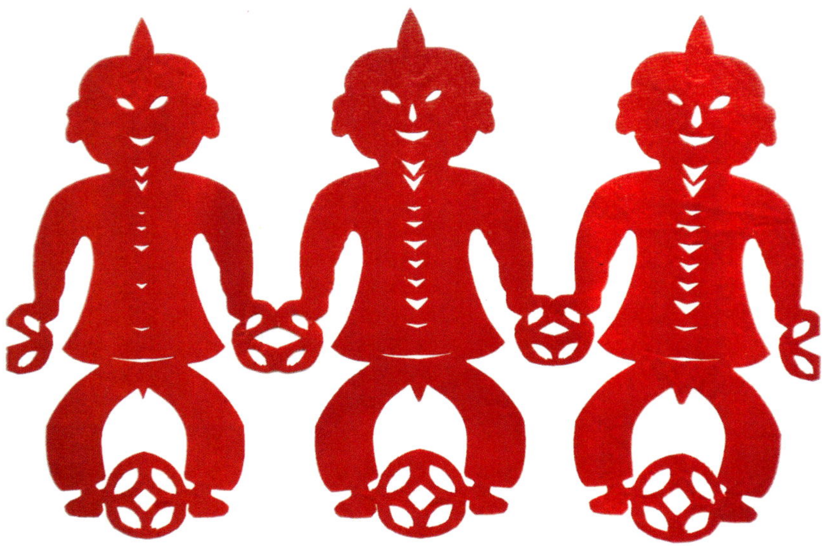

The Moppet Exorcising Evil

This kind of evil-exorcising moppet is also called a "money-grabbing moppet" or a "ghost-sending moppet." There is an old saying that "ghosts come to ask for money, so they can be sent away with money, and then disasters can be eliminated and diseases gotten rid of." Therefore people cut a "money-grabbing moppet" and burn it. In this way they "send" money to the ghosts to pray for safety.

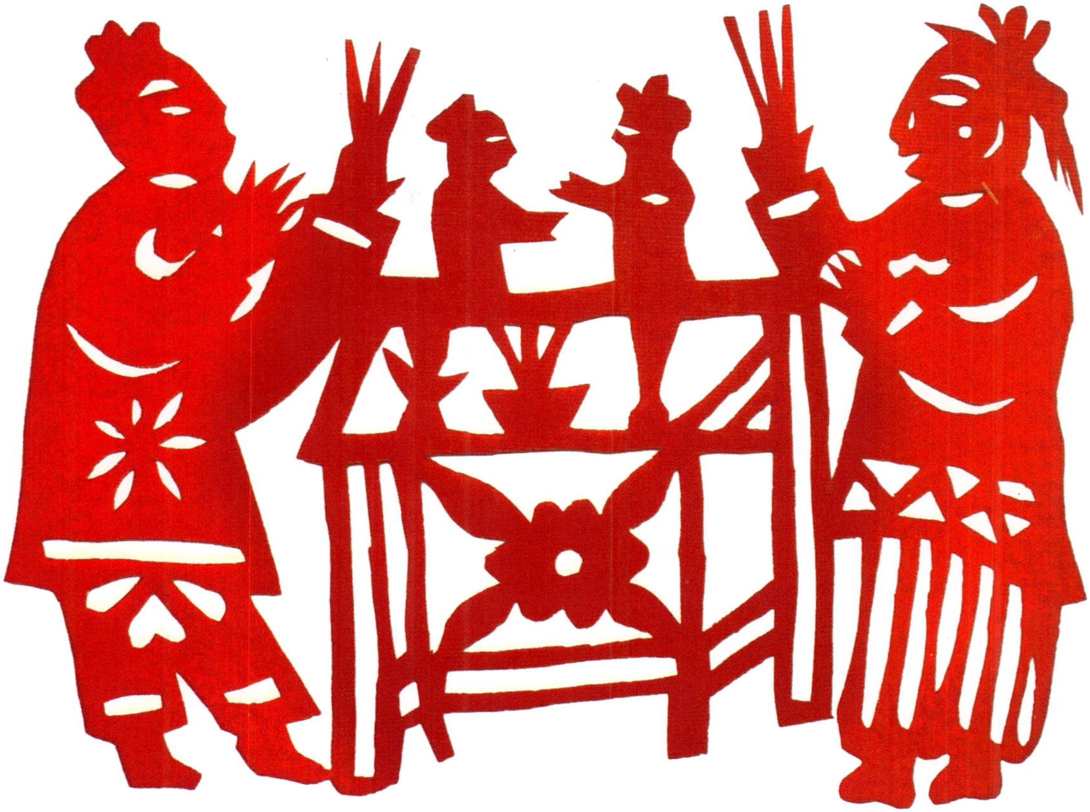

House Safety

A long time ago, in remote areas, if families and livestock were not healthy or there was something bad happening, the housewife would make a paper-cut (the women on the left and right side of the paper hold three joss sticks worshipping heaven, earth and their ancestors; the two small people on the altar in the paper symbolize all the deities). She would then walk around the house three times with the paper-cut in her hands. When she finished she burned the paper-cut and threw it in a bowl of clear water while saying "Heaven, earth and our ancestors, please show your magic powers to exorcise evil and ward off disasters in order to keep the family safe" again and again. Holding the bowl she would walk out the gate and when she came to the road, she spilled the water with the ashes and then went back saying the same words over and over on the way. After the people in the paper-cut were burned and changed into immortals they would exorcise evil and eliminate disasters to keep the family safe.

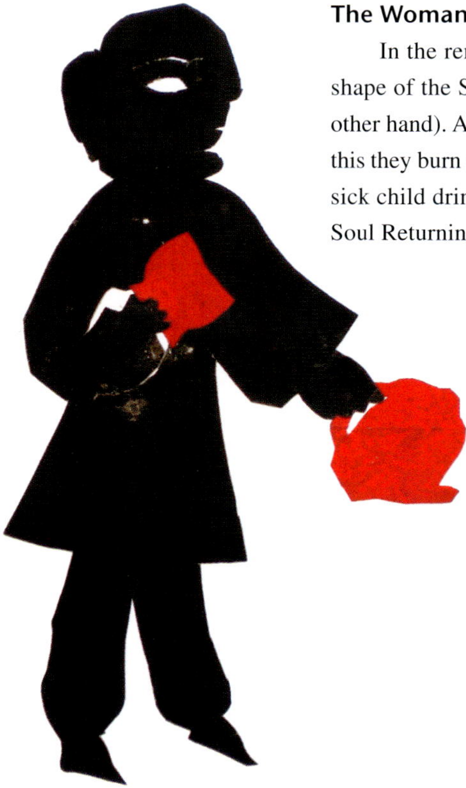

The Woman Returning a Soul

In the remote countryside, if a child is sick, someone will make a paper-cut in the shape of the Soul-Returning Woman (who holds water in one hand and medicine in the other hand). A parent holds the paper and moves it around the sick child three times. After this they burn the paper and put the ashes into a bowl of clear water and mix it up. Then the sick child drinks the water and this is said to be able to get rid of the illness because the Soul Returning Woman is the goddess Nuwa.

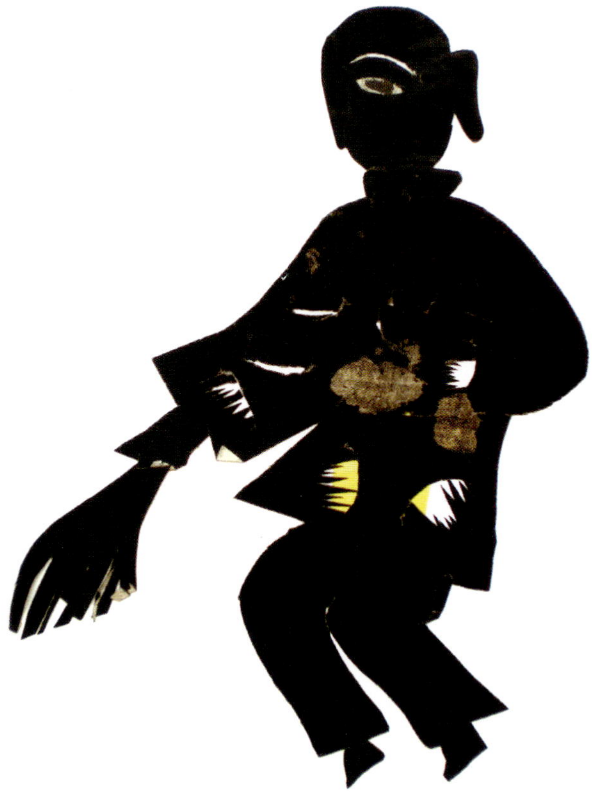

The Woman Calling Back a Soul

The purpose of this paper-cut is similar to that of the above one. This one is especially for the children who always cry or are lazy or hate to eat food because they are scared. For any of these symptoms the people regard the child as having "lost their soul because of fright." Therefore they make a paper-cut in the shape of the Soul-Calling-Back Woman who holds a broom in one hand and a dustpan in the other hand to waken, sweep up and call back the lost soul.

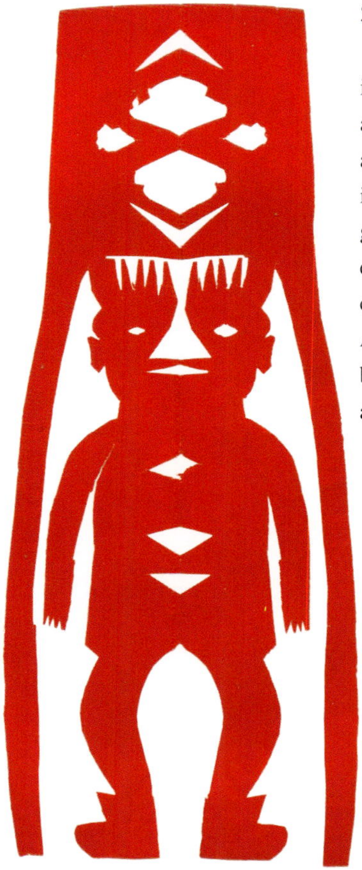

Streamer Calling Back a Soul

Methods of using paper-cuts to evoke the soul and get rid of illness are largely identical but with minor differences. Normally a family member ignites the paper-cut and moves it around the sick child while murmuring such words as "burning the paper and moving it around, all illnesses and evils run away" over and over. When the paper is burnt it is thrown into a bowl of clear water. After that the person holds the bowl and goes outside while chanting "burning the paper to display magic power which exorcises evil and gets rid of illness to keep us safe and healthy." They spill the water at the crossing and then return all the time chanting and calling the name of the sick child. After returning they shake the bowl in the direction of the sick child and say "please go back to the body quickly, please go back to the body quickly." They then put the bowl at the bedside of the child. After all of this they think that the illness will be cured.

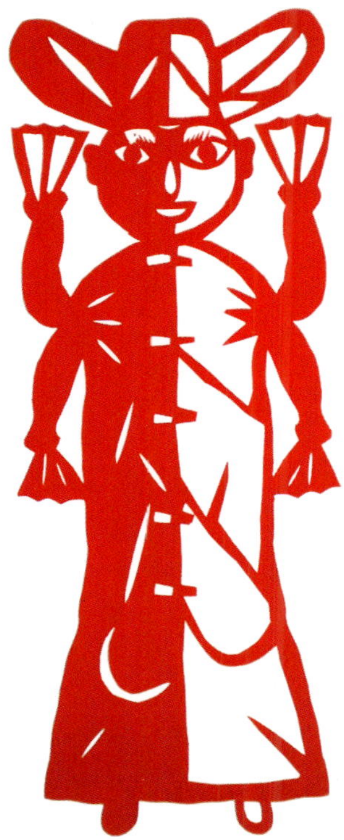

Yin and *Yang*

This kind of paper-cut is also used to call back the soul for the very ill person, with the wish of calling the ill person back to this world from the *Yin* and *Yang* world.

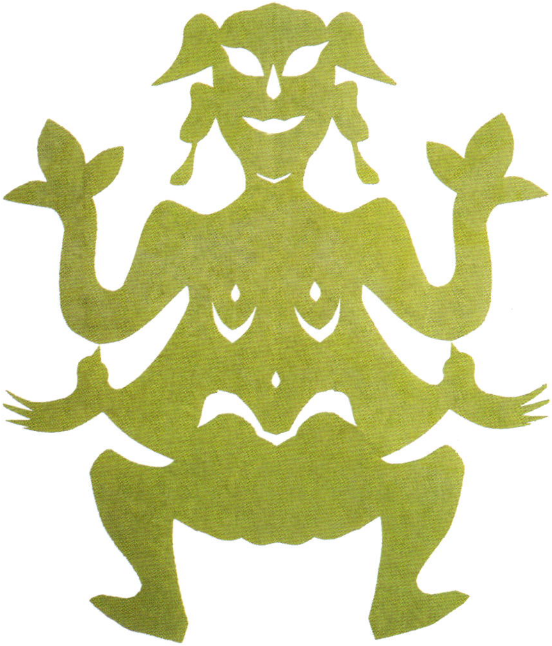

A Moppet Exorcising Evil

The person in the paper-cut holds a peach in each of his hands.The peaches are believed to be able to subdue evil while a pair of male birds standing on each side of the garment of the person can also keep evil away.

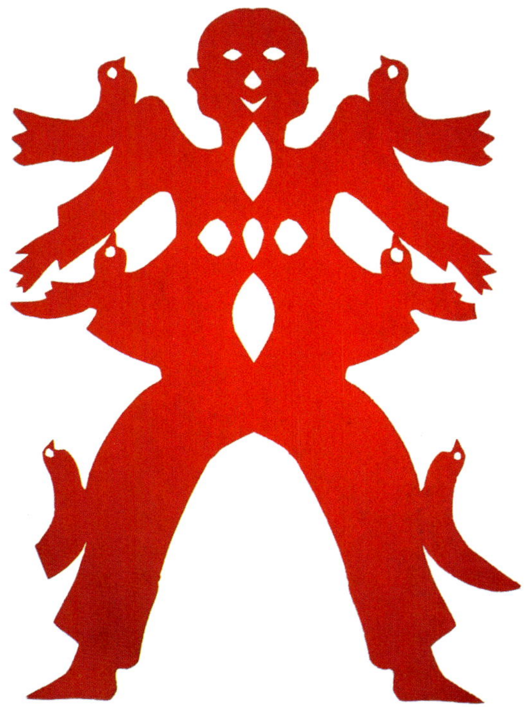

An Evil Subduing Moppet

This work is similar to the above in terms of purpose, but the person is male and is stretching his legs. It is similar to the Chinese character "大," or "天" or "夫" in shape. Moreover, there are six birds standing on each side of the person. The person, the character and the birds are all masculine so the combination is more powerful in exorcising evil.

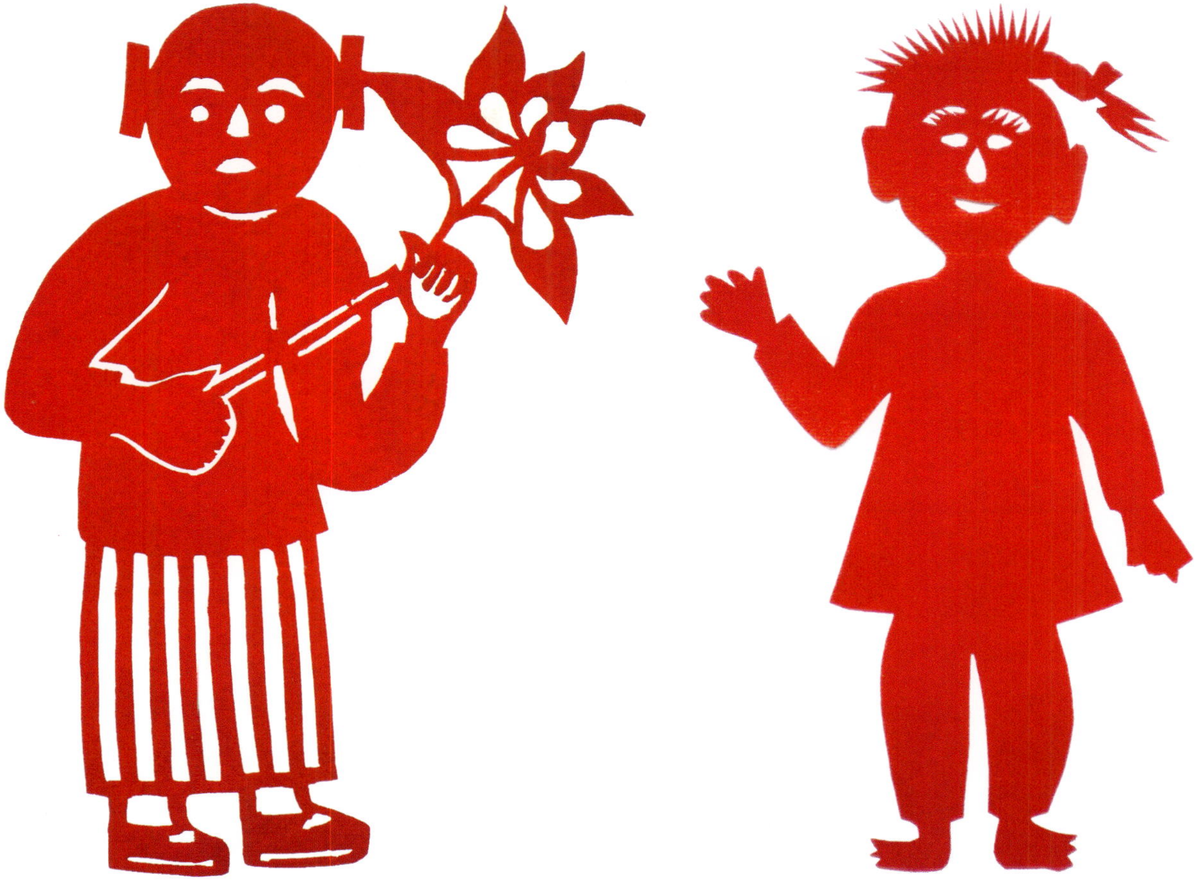

A Moppet Calling Back a Soul

This is used for a frightened child and has a red thread tied to the top of the paper-cut so as to find the illness. Someone lifts the moppet and walks around calling the name of the sick child. They then go back, also calling the name of the sick child and say "go home." After going back home they put the paper-cut moppet under the pillow of the sick child. In this way, they think the soul will go back to the body and the illness will be cured.

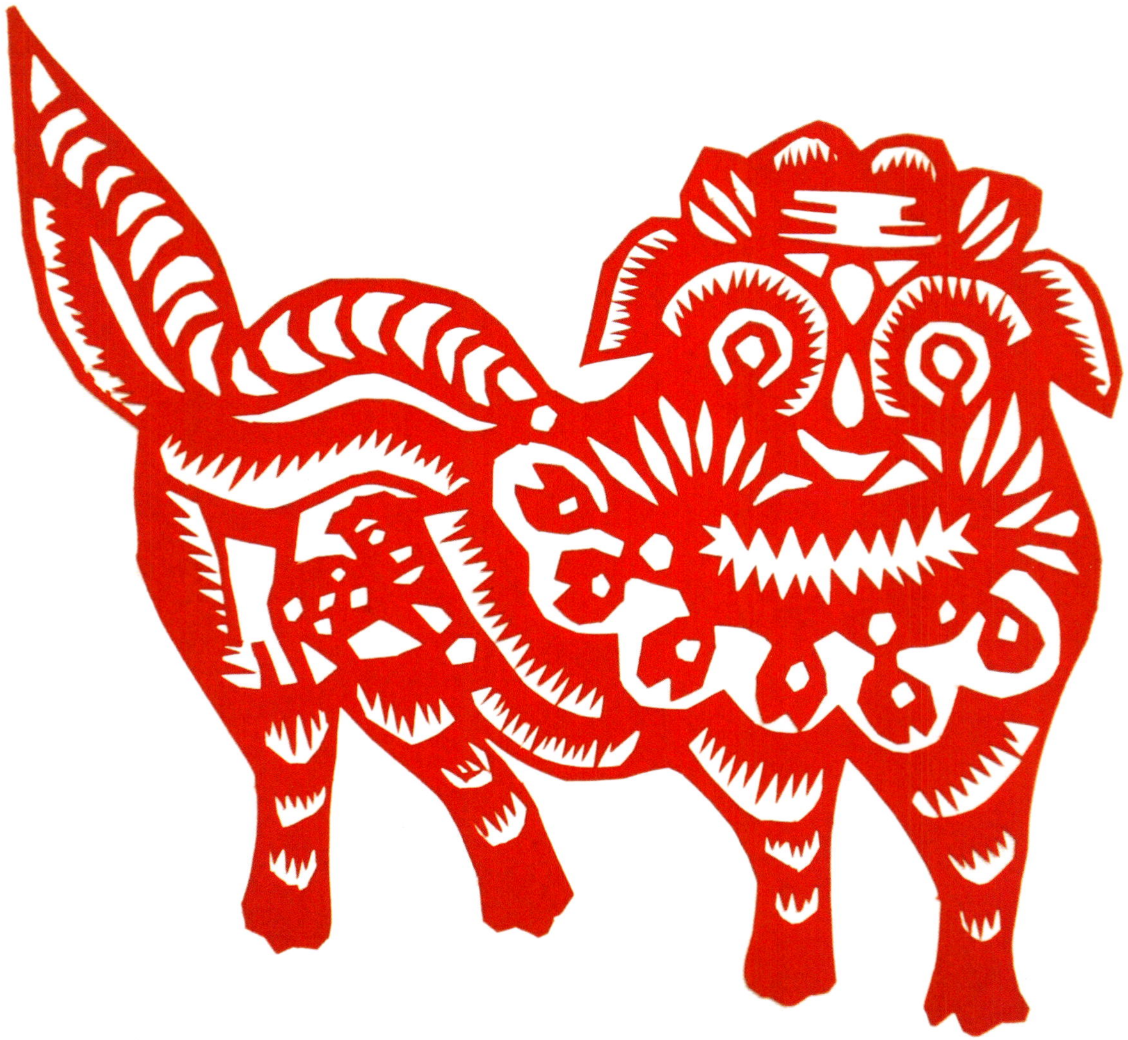

A Fierce Tiger Guarding a House

In the traditional folk concept the tiger is ingenious and able to keep evil away. Hence, making a paper-cut of a fierce tiger with red paper is considered to be able to prevent evil and can surely keep the family safe and healthy.

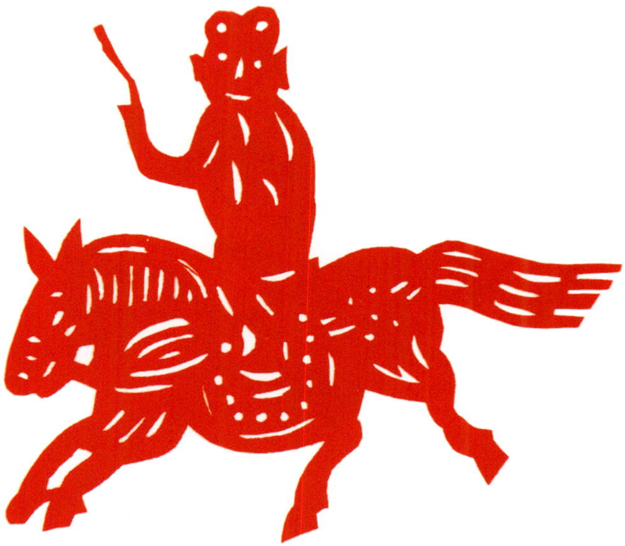

A Moppet Calling Back a Soul

People make a paper-cut in the shape of a person riding a horse to regain the soul back to the body quickly so as to get rid of an illness.

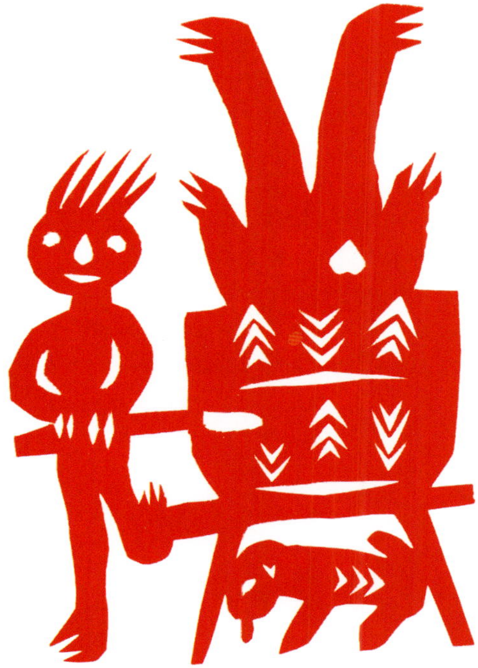

Subduing Ghosts

Most people think that when they die their souls will go to the nether world. There are good and bad people in this world and good and bad ghosts in the nether world. This paper-cut work is a subdued evil ghost sentenced to "the death penalty" by an official in the nether world.The said official also sends spirites to grind the subducd evil ghost to nothing, thus it can no longer do evil things.

This kind of paper-cut is normally burned in the course of ceremonies for subduing ghosts, exorcising evil and getting rid of illness. This kind of ceremony is very superstitious.

A Divine Tiger Subduing Evil

This is a tale recorded in ancient books. In the distant past there was an enormous peach tree with a spread of 1,500 km. A golden rooster stood on the tree taking charge of heralding the break of a day. Under the tree crouched a divine tiger who was in charging of eating evil ghosts. Hence, folk people cut a divine tiger to subdue evil.

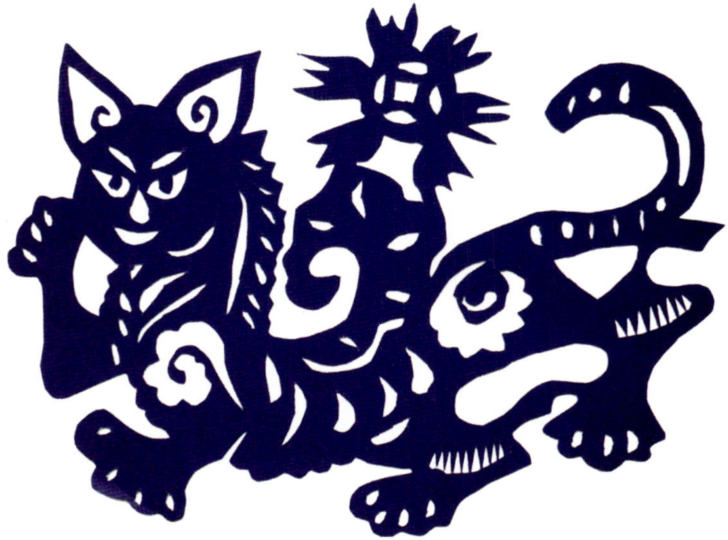

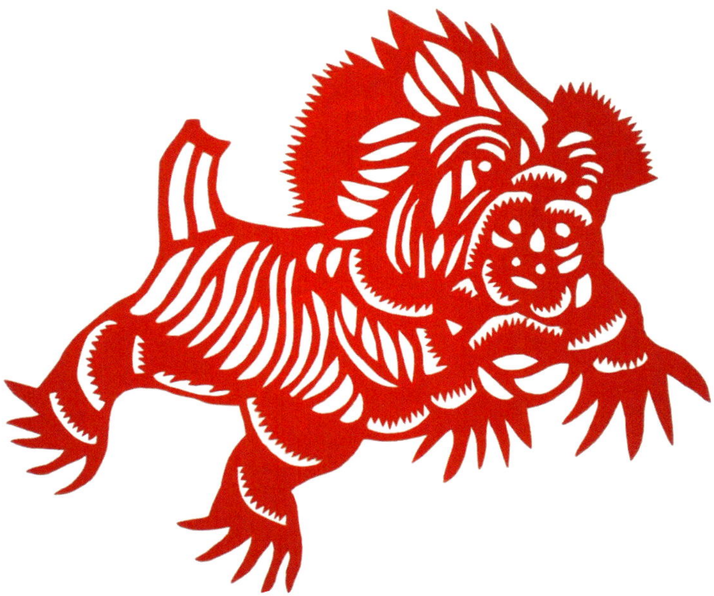

A Fierce Tiger Exorcising Evil

(ibid)

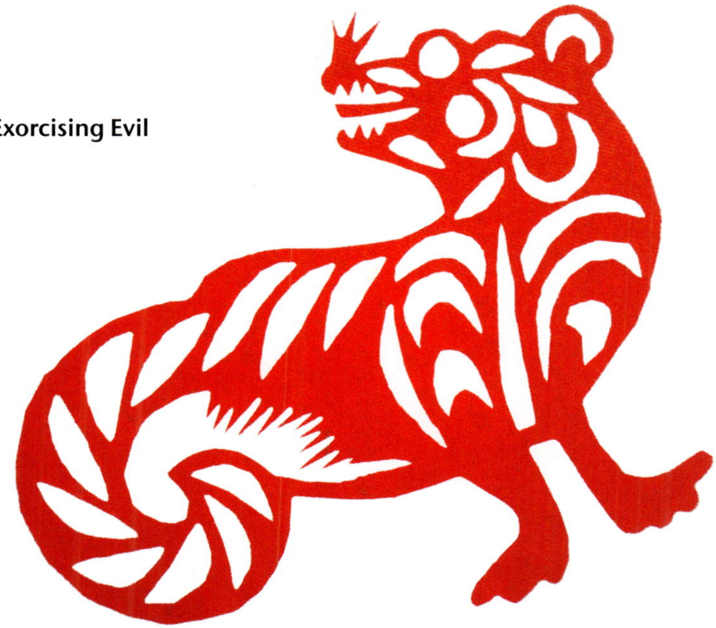

A Fierce Tiger Exorcising Evil
(ibid)

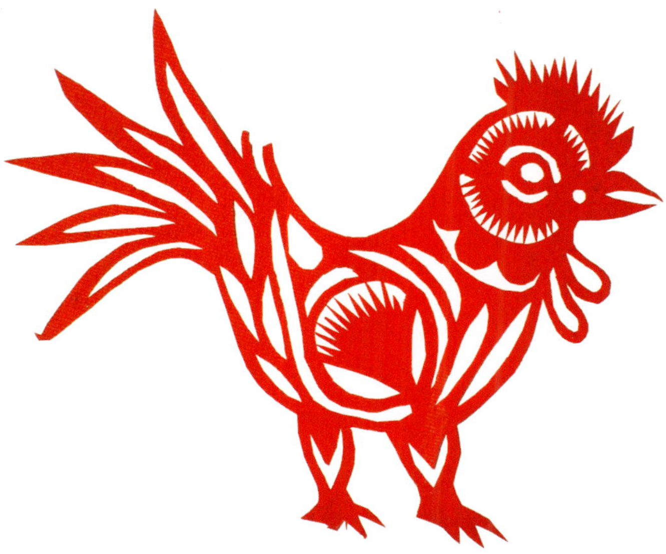

A Rooster Guarding the House

"Now the rooster has crowed and all under heaven is bright." The rooster is always connected with the sun, dawn, day break and the male. In the folk concept, *yin* and *yang* restrict each other mutually and good prevails over evil. All evil is afraid of sunshine. Hence, pasting a paper-cut rooster should exorcise evil and guard the house.

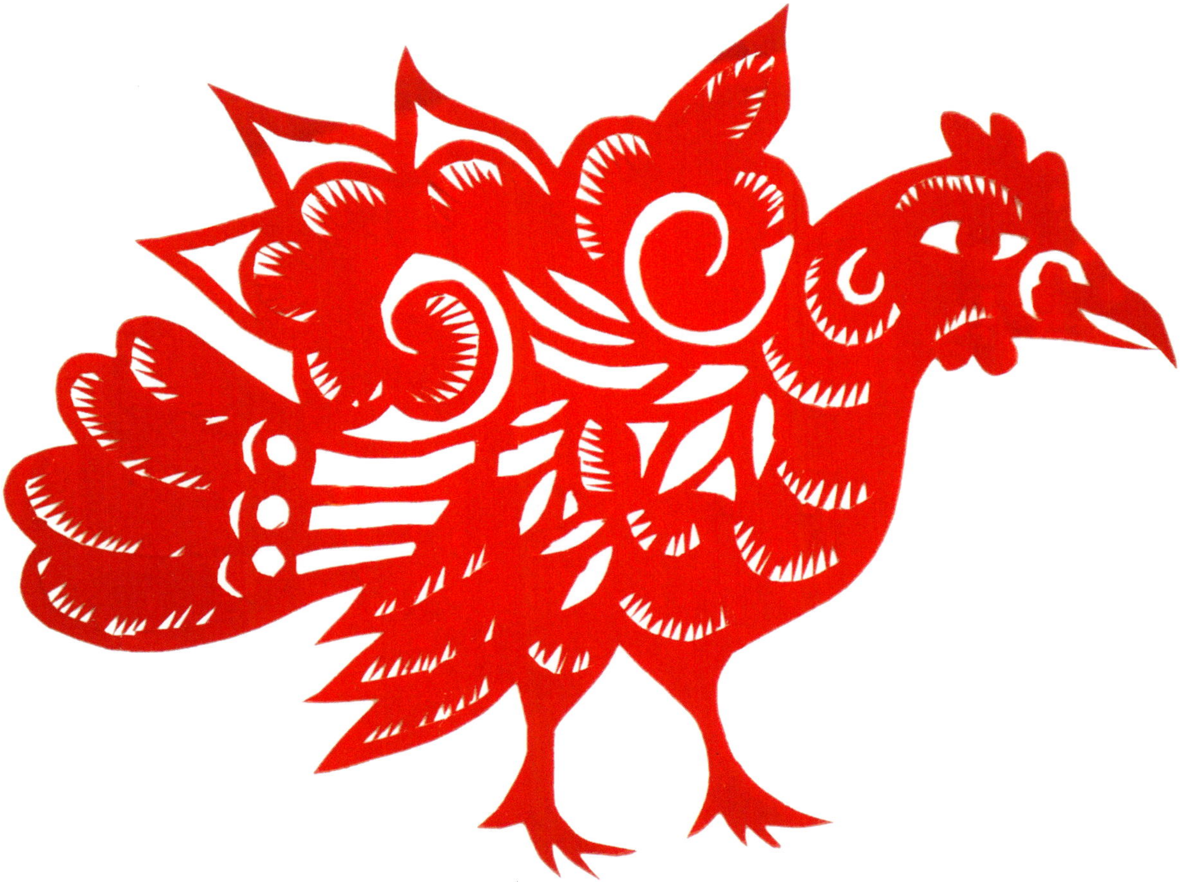

A Rooster Eating the Five Poisonous Creatures

The rooster is a symbol of masculinity. It is fond of eating insects, scorpions and centipedes. Hence, when the different poisonous insects come out around the fifth day of the fifth lunar month and injure children, people cut a rooster to paste on the door so as to exorcise these poisonous creatures.

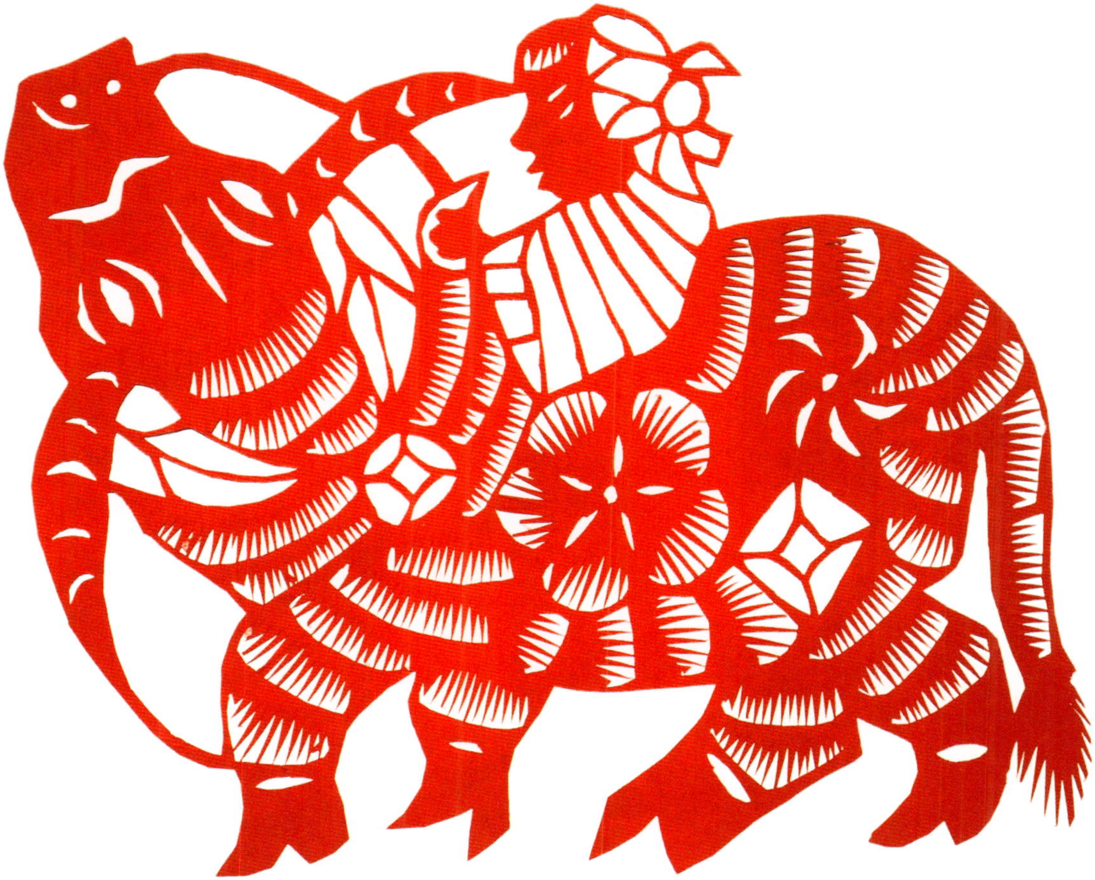

A Black Ox Expelling Plague

A country ballad goes like this, "On the 23rd day of the first lunar month, Laozi comes to give out pills. A black ox paper-cut is pasted on the door especially subduing sprites." It is said that Laozi comes to areas of Henan and Shaanxi riding a black ox on a purple cloud to give out pills and expel plagues. Hence, the black ox is said to be able to expel plagues.

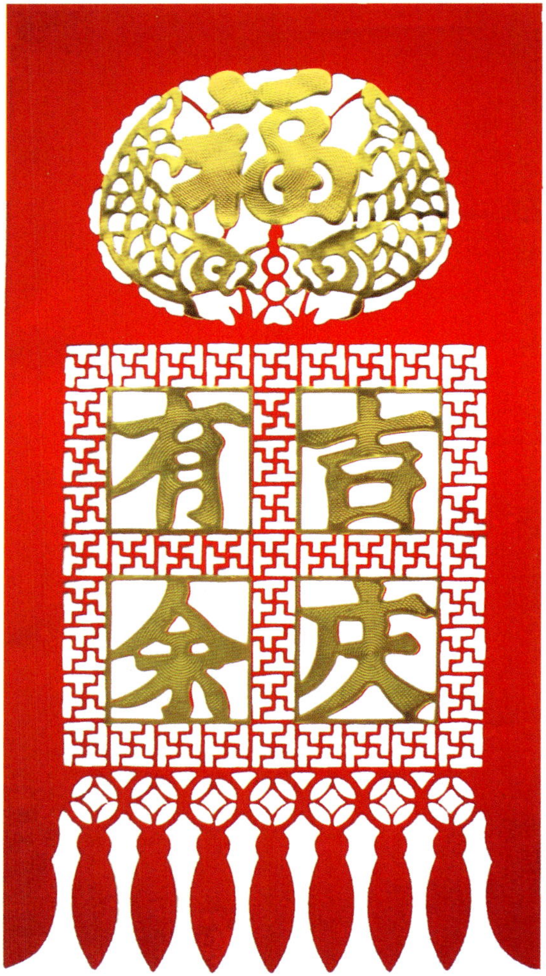

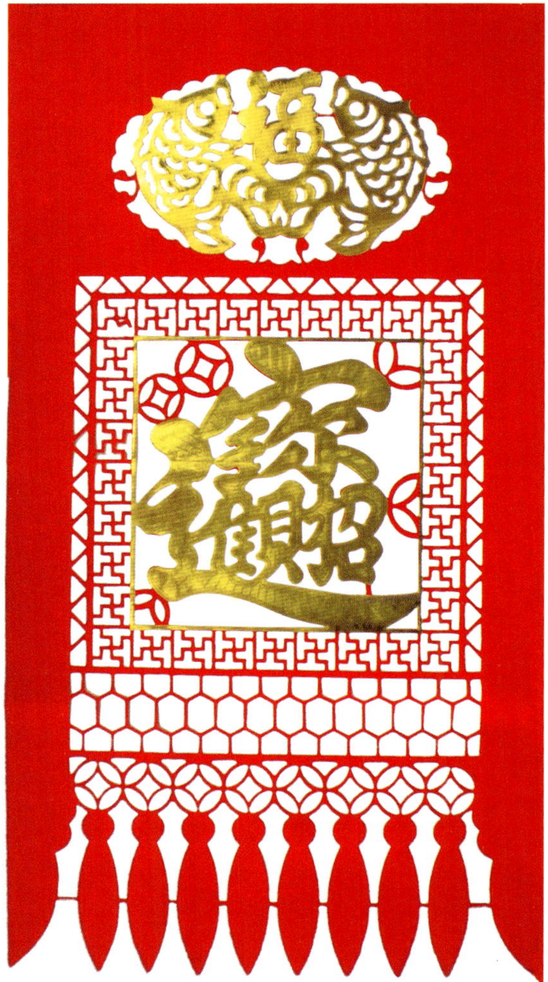

Good Luck and Abundance

This work is a streamer pasted on the door jamb by each household during the Spring Festival.

Treasures Filling the Home

(ibid)

Category of Gifts

Modern commercial economy attaches great importance to the external packaging of gifts. It seems that the gifts with the more luxurious packaging are more expensive and valuable even though the gift inside is the same. Such packaging is neither economical nor a blessing. According to Chinese traditional courtesy, the gifts sent to and from friends and relatives on festivals or big events did not have such packaging. People added a self-made paper-cut which had the relevant theme with the activity and the gift. This not only added colour to the gift giving but also expressed the wishes of the gift-sender. The true sentiment expressed in a paper-cut makes it more valuable to the person it is given to.

For example: when sending gifts to older people on their birthday, people make a paper-cut in the shape of a big peach and add the Zodiac animal of that year on the peach. It gives great pleasure to the older person to receive a paper-cut with their gift. It is completely in line with the theme of celebrating their birthday and also expresses the wish for them to have a long life.

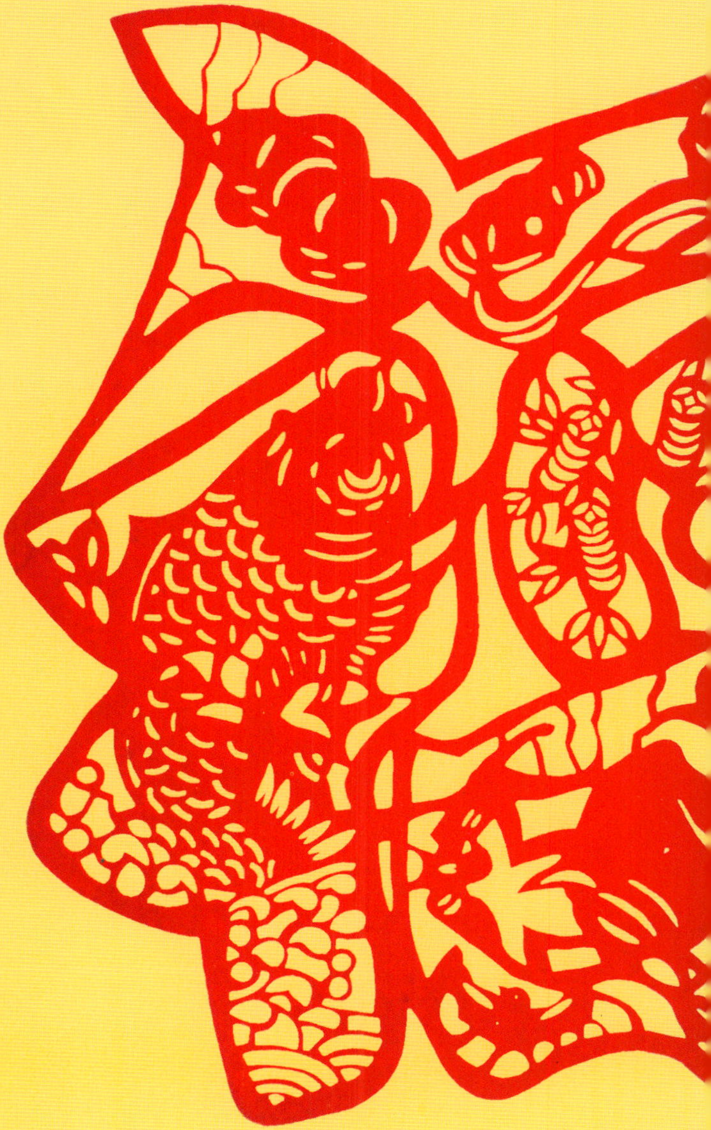

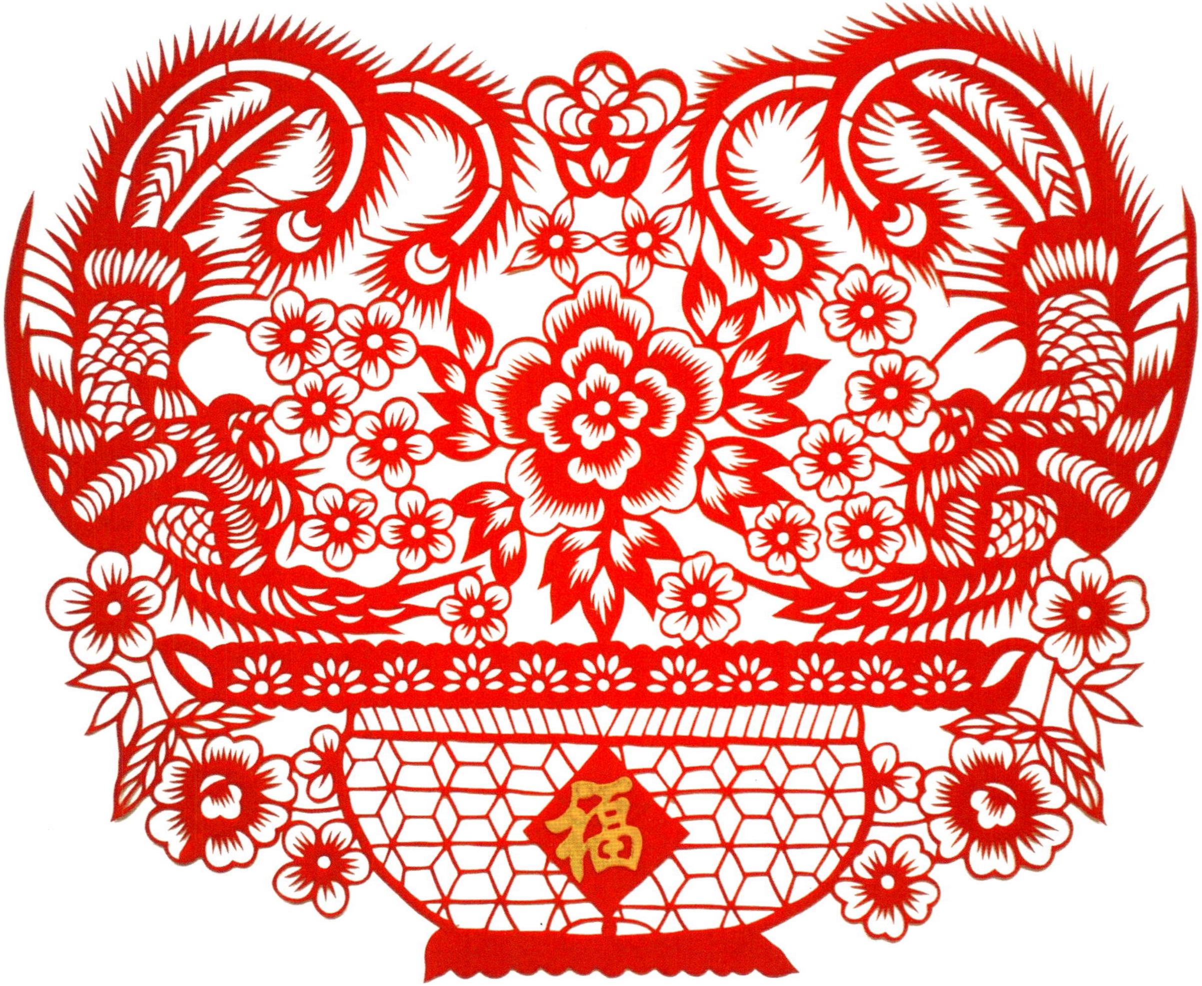

The Phoenix and a Peony

This is a paper-cut picture which is put with the gifts for a wedding. The "Phoenix and a peony" carry the meaning that the couple will be happy and have a good life together.

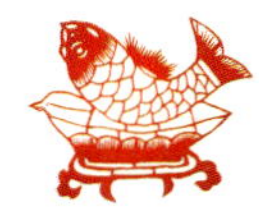

Good Luck and Abundance

In Chinese the word meaning fish and the word meaning abundance have the same pronunciation. Hence, a fish when used in folk craftwork always has the meaning of abundance. This one and the following three are mostly put on sacrificial food or on a food box.

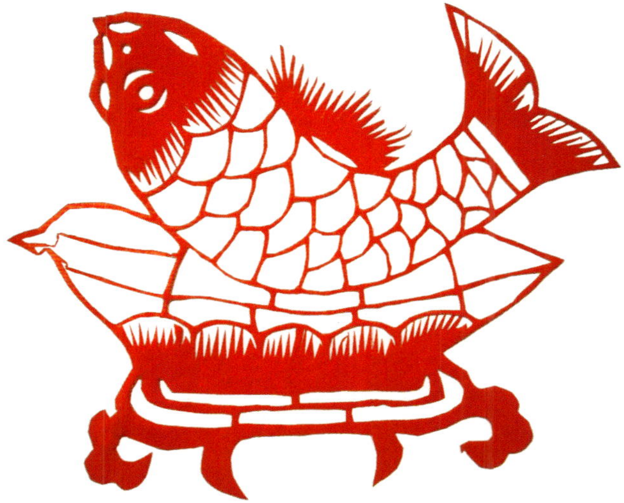

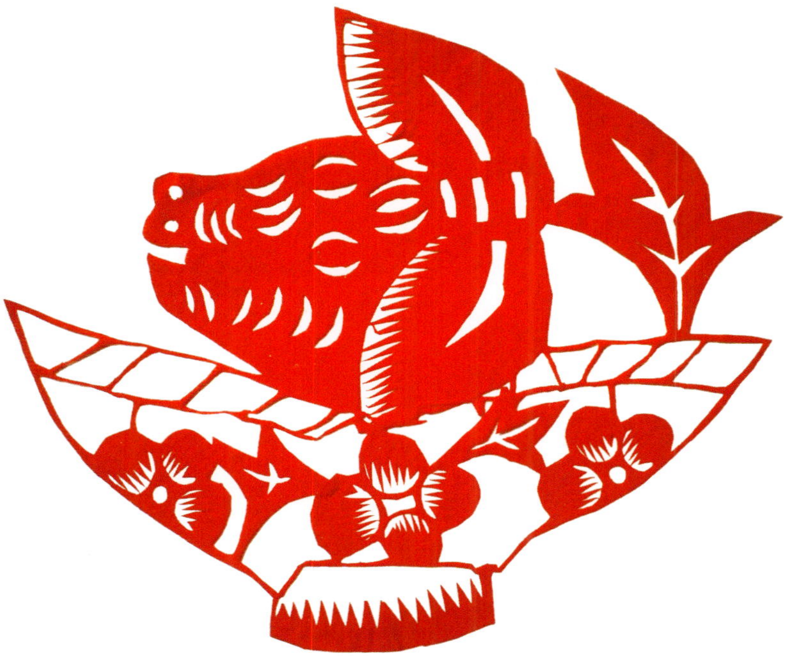

The Hog's Head

A hog's head is necessary to make a traditional sacrifice. Hence, a hog's head paper-cut will add meaning to the sacrificial offerings.

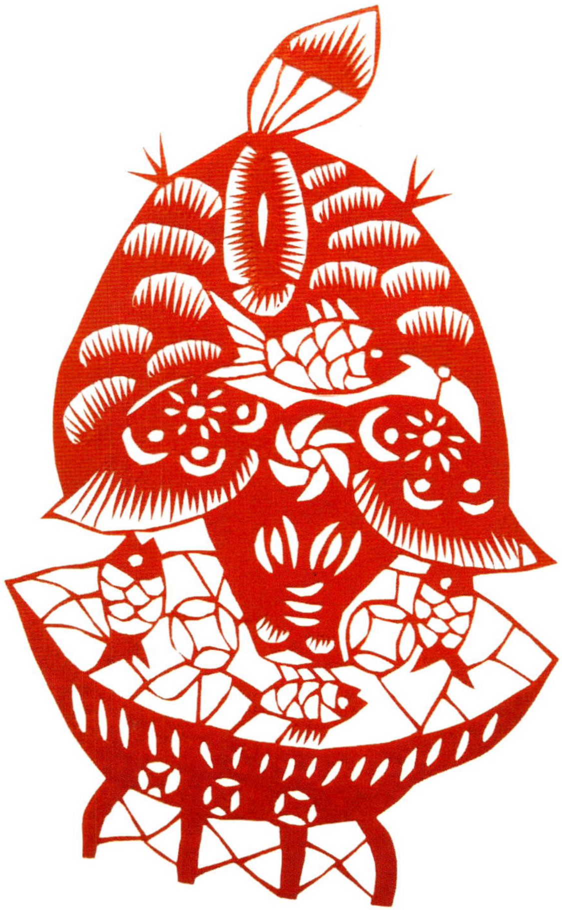

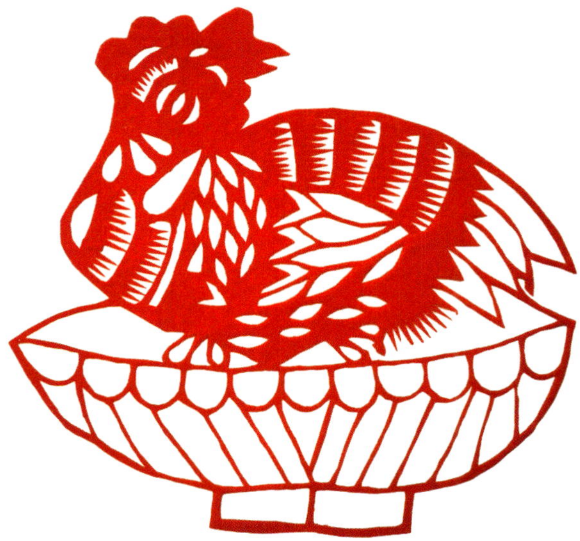

The Hog

Pork can be cooked in many different way. In a grand sacrificial ceremony putting this picture on a hog will interest people a lot. The fish and money designs in the picture wish abundance and wealth.

Luck

The Chinese words meaning cock and luck have the same pronunciation "*Ji*," so the appearance of a cock indicates luck. Putting this picture on a box of food will bring luck to people.

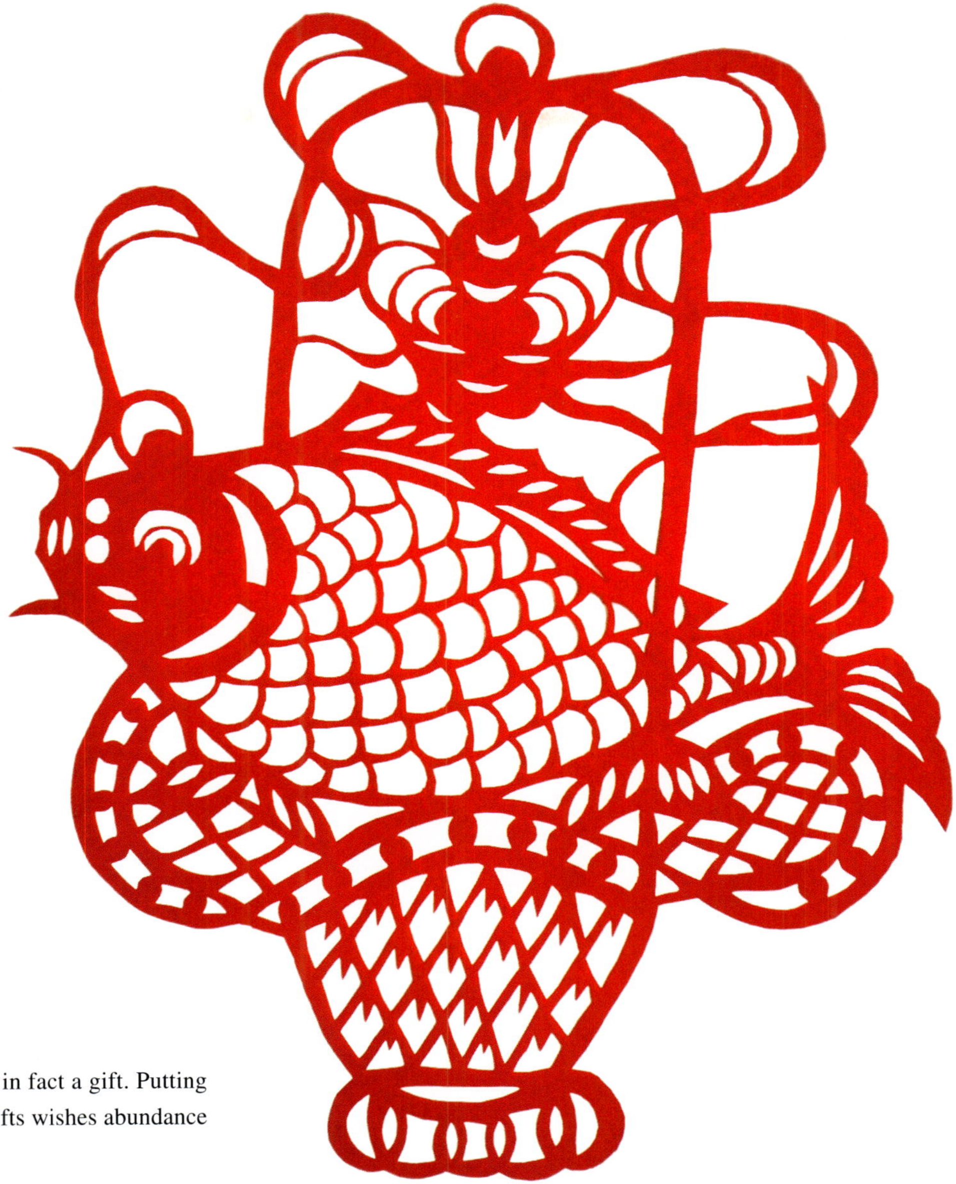

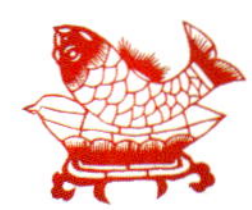

A Basket of Fish

A basket of fish is in fact a gift. Putting this picture of fish on gifts wishes abundance for people.

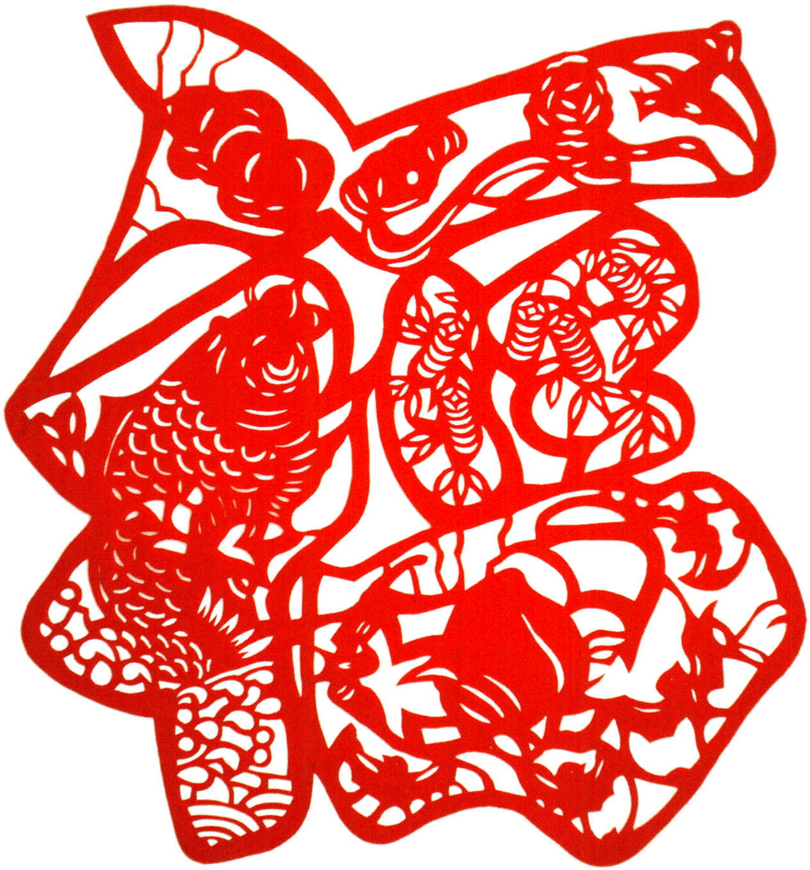

The Chinese Character "*Fu*"（福）

"*Fu*" in Chinese means "good luck" and "happiness." In this picture "*Fu*" is comprised of several parts. The fish on its left symbolizes abundance. The "S-shaped sceptre" hidden in the horizontal stroke on the right wishes everything goes well. The middle part on the right side is comprised of "money trees." " 田 "(field) at the bottom of the right part of the word is composed of five bats and a longevity peach, implying "good health and longevity." On the eve of festivals it is good to send several such pictures to relatives and friends to express good wishes.

The Chinese animal signs are a 12-year cycle used for dating the years. They represent a cyclical concept of time, rather than the Western linear concept of time. In the Chinese calendar, the beginning of the year falls somewhere between late January and early February. The 12 Zodiac animals are respectively Rat, Ox, Tiger, Rabbit, Dragon, Snake, Horse, Sheep, Monkey, Rooster, Dog and Pig. The following 12 pictures are the "Zodiac animals" put on gifts for celebrating others' birthdays.

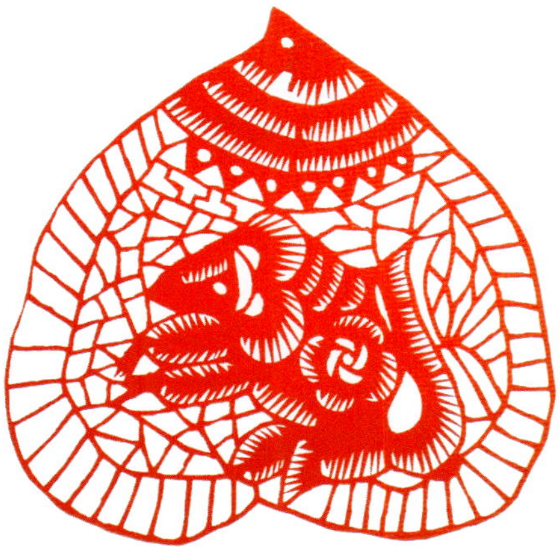

A Peach and a Rat

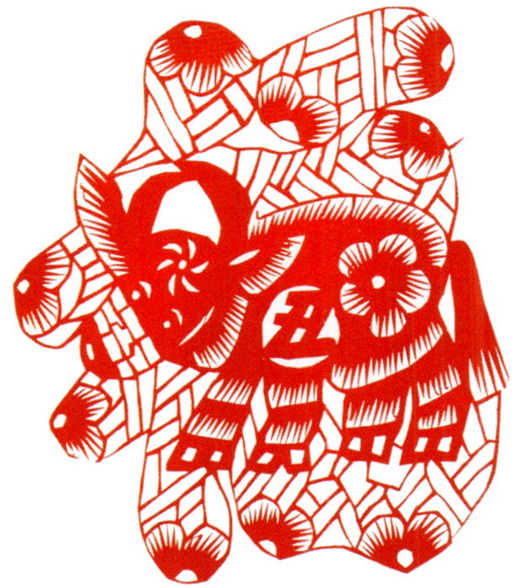

A Lucky Ox

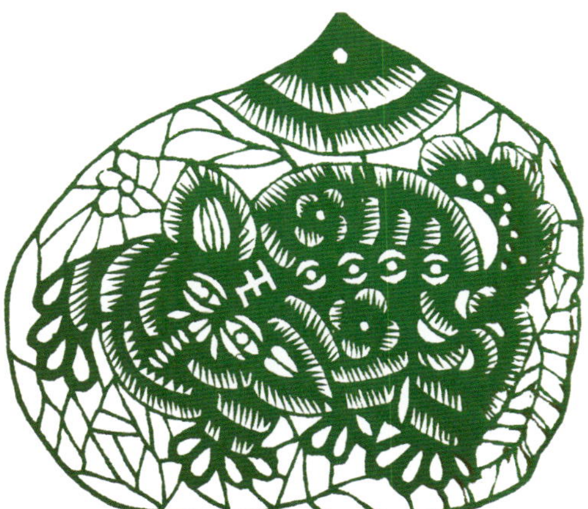

A Peach and a Tiger

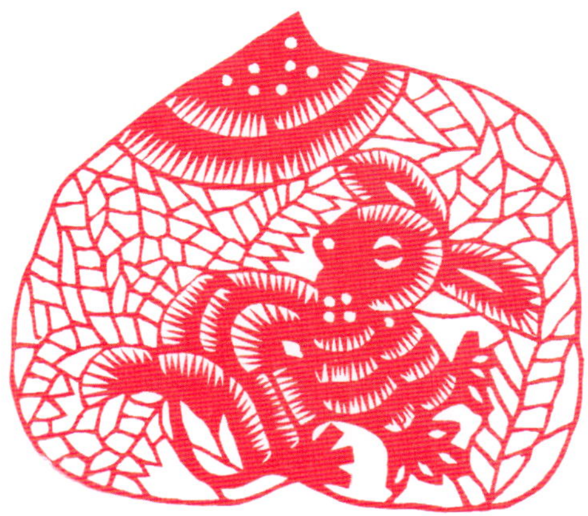

A Peach and a Rabbit

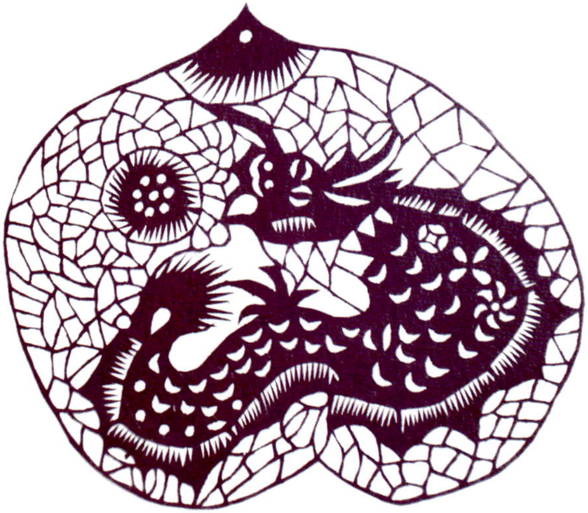

A Peach and a Dragon

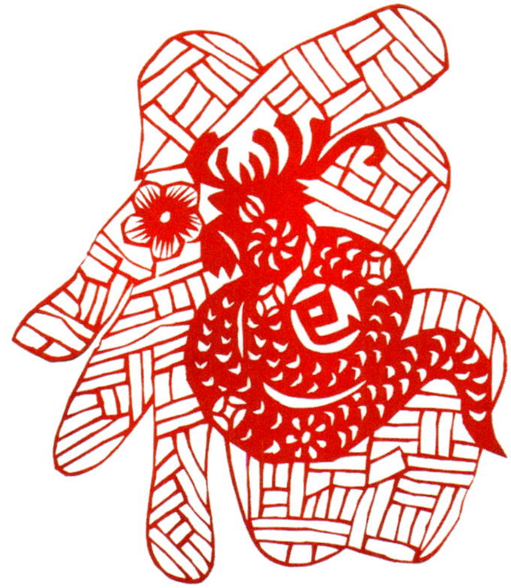

A Lucky Snake

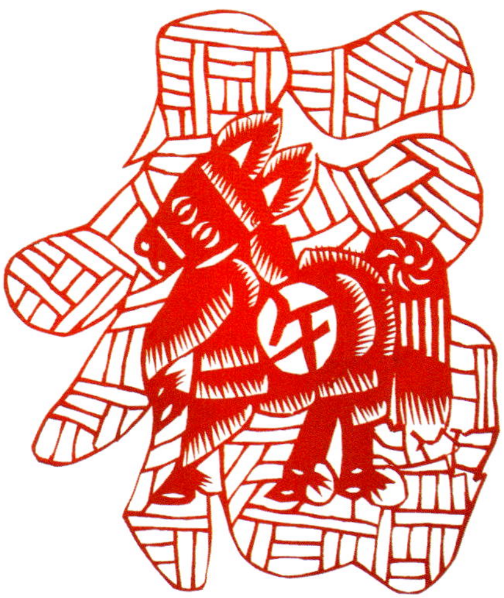

A Lucky Horse

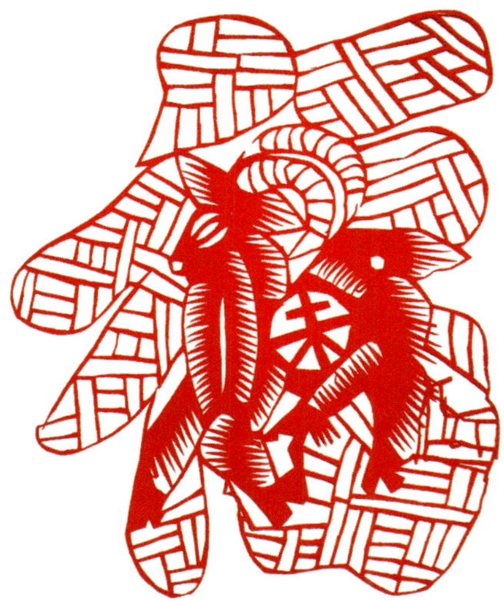

A Lucky Sheep

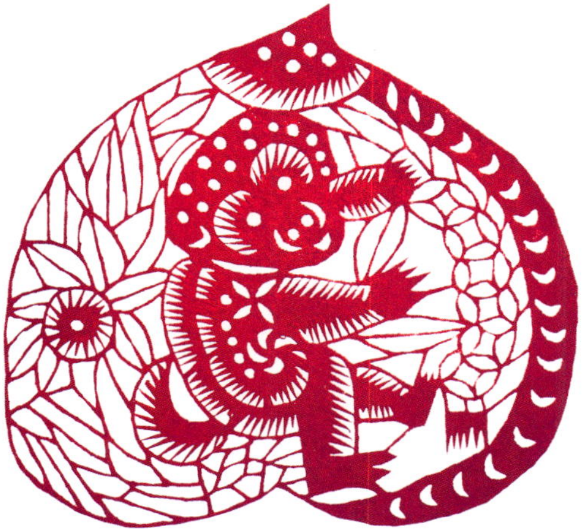

A Peach and a Monkey

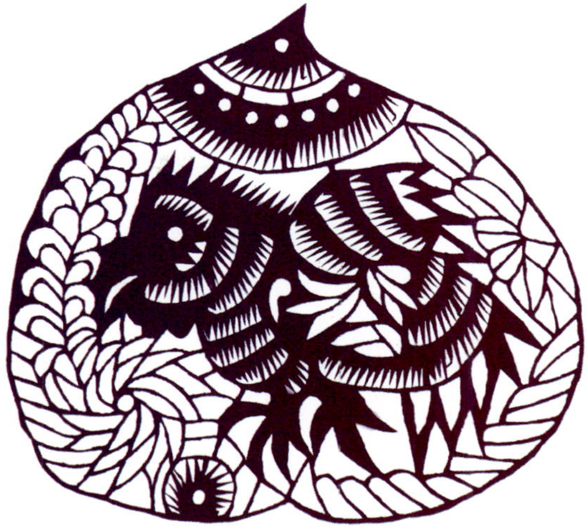

A Peach and a Rooster

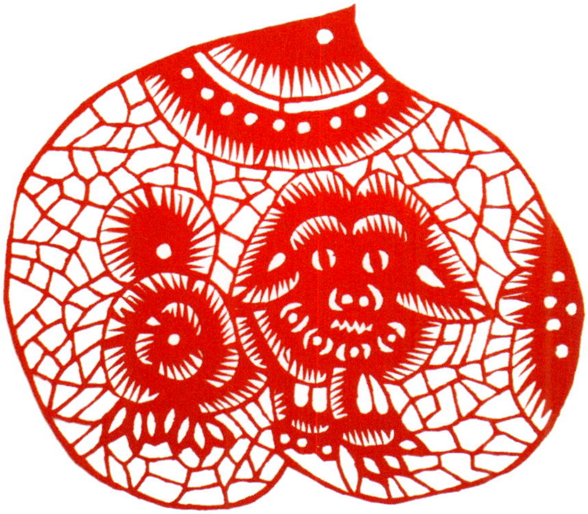

A Peach and a Dog

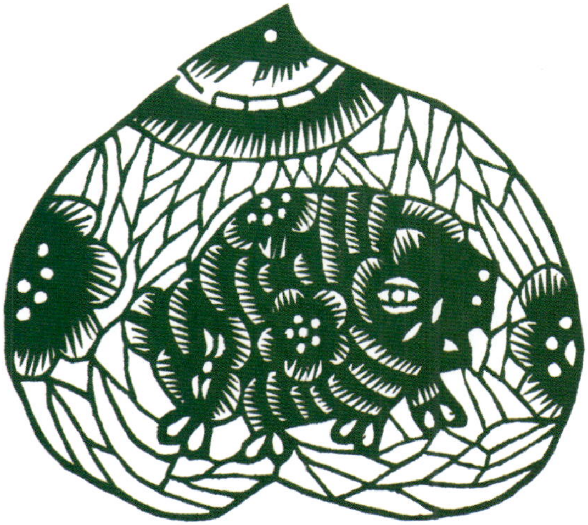

A Peach and a Pig

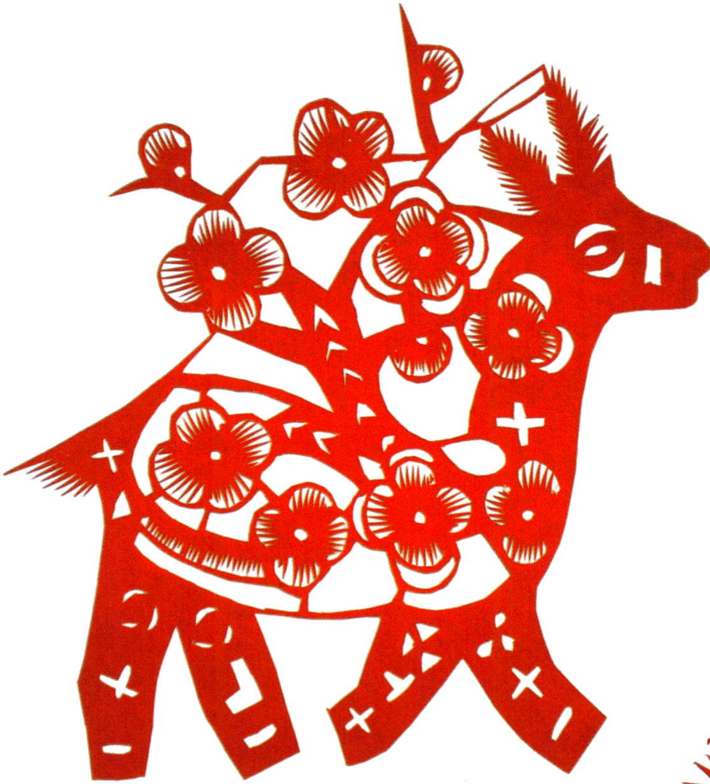

The Sika

The pinetree, crane and deer have long lives. Hence, a sika cutting to put with the gift and sent to an older person wishes them a long life.

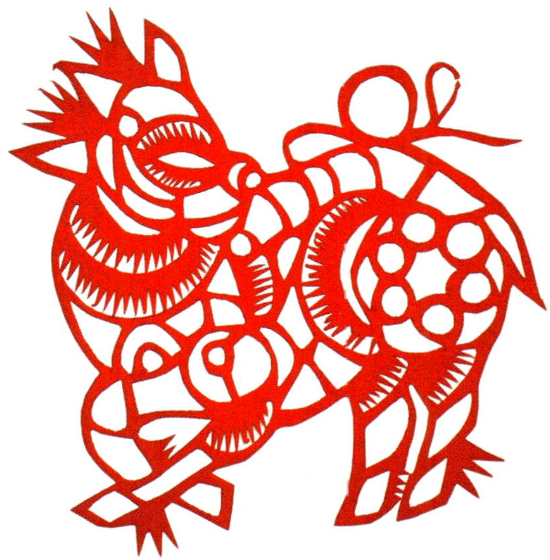

The Sika
(ibid)

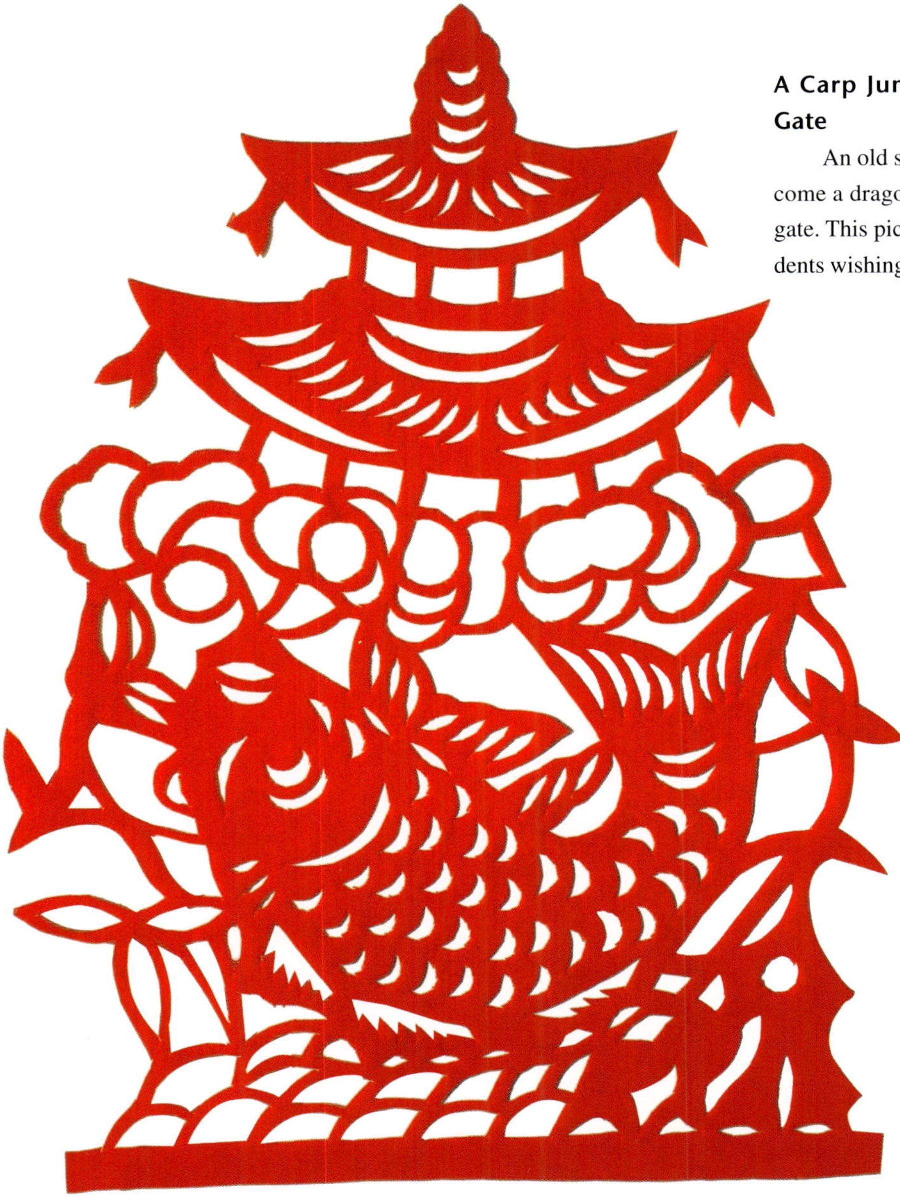

A Carp Jumping Over the Dragon Gate

An old story tells that a carp could become a dragon if it leaped over the dragon gate. This picture is put on gifts sent to students wishing them success in their studies.

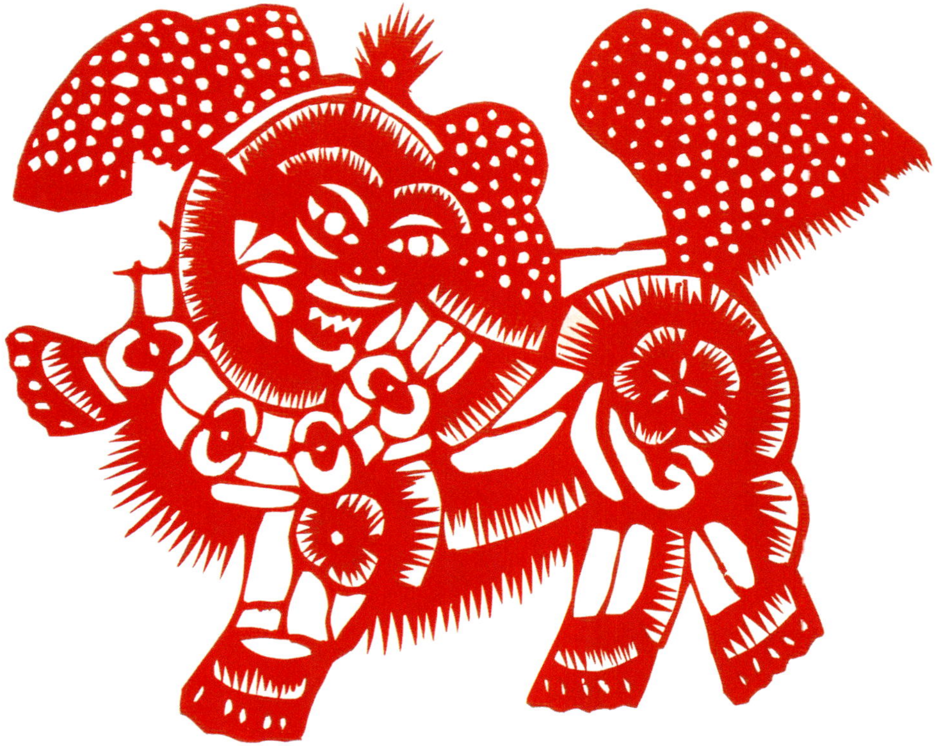

The Happy Lion

An old woman in northern Shaanxi Province has preserved more than 100 master copies of paper-cut lions in recent years. Some are powerful, some gentle and quiet, some shake their heads and smile fatuously, some are upright and solemn, some look like kind old people and some look piquant and lovely like a child. I asked her, " Have you ever seen real lion?" She replied, " No, I heard it hurt people. But I will not cut it.What I cut is the lion in my mind." Curiously, I asked again, "What do lions in your mind look like?" She replied sincerely, "Haven't you ever heard? Nine out of ten lions are leaders. What an honour! In old times the highest-ranking official was the Grand Tutor (in Chinese, it has the same pronunciation as the word lion). Nowadays the people with talent and knowledge are engineers and teachers (ibid, they also have the same pronunciation with the word lion in Chinese). How noble! You see that lion laugh with the mouth happy? How happy! Hence, I would like to cut an imposing, noble and happy lion to send to others." Those words completely explain the ancient people's purpose and principle of creating figures. It is to express wishes which is also a feature of the Chinese traditional plastic arts.

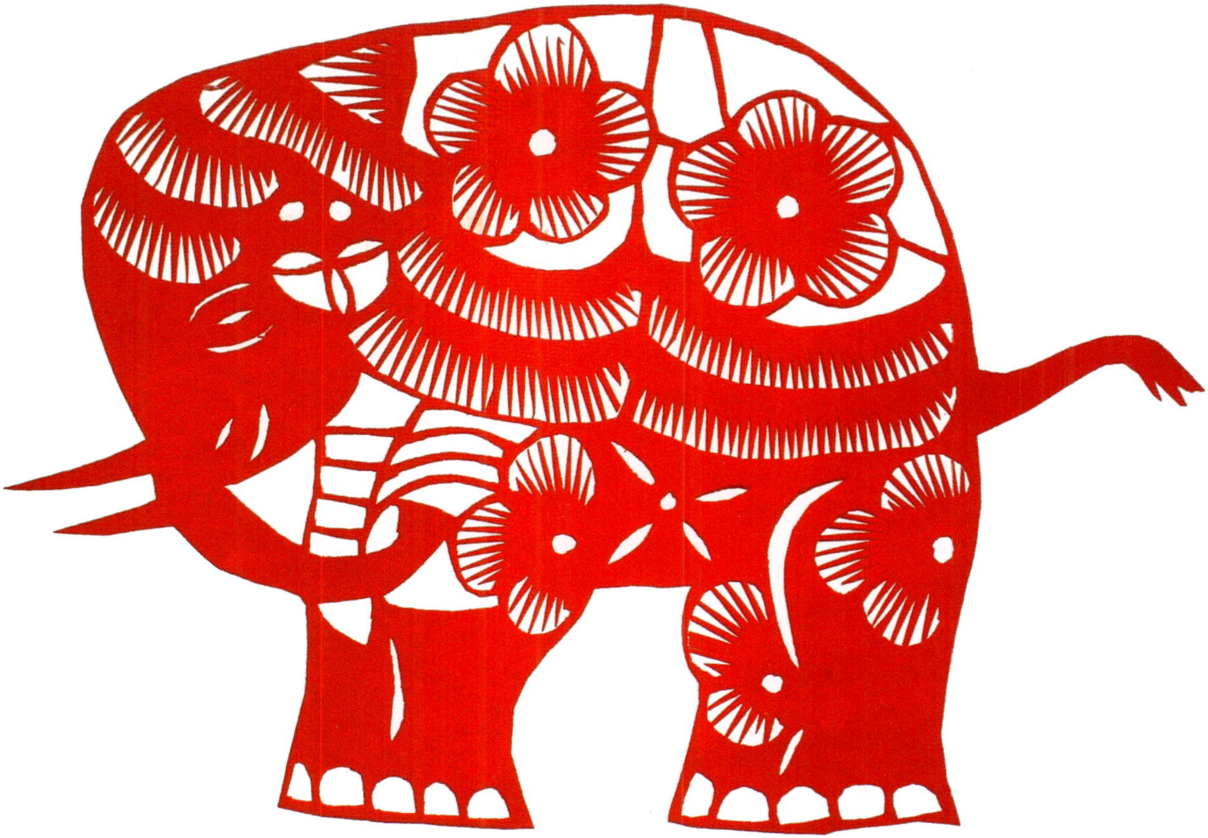

Everything Looks Fresh

This is a picture put on gifts for the Spring Festival, wishing a fresh New Year.

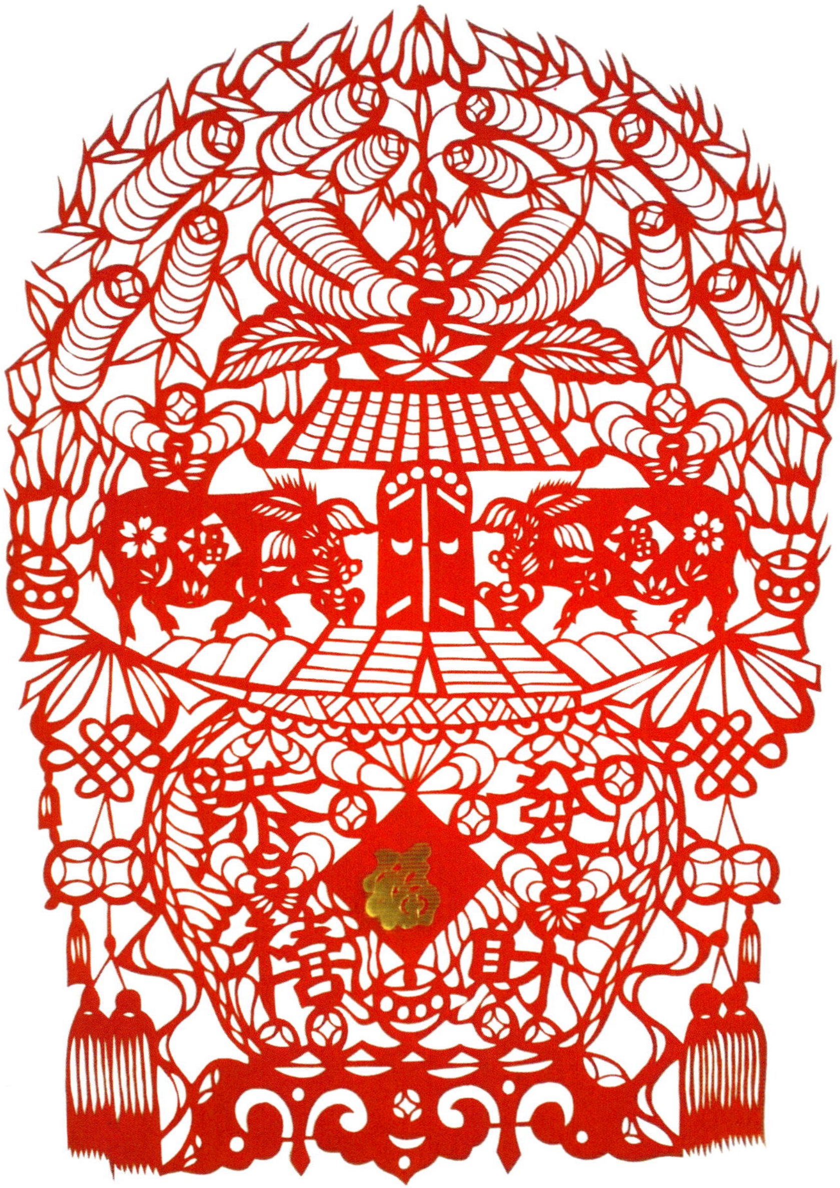

A Hog Knocking at the Door

Bristles can be made into a brush and skin into leather. Pork can be eaten and its excrement is high-quality farm manure. Hence, the hog is a treasure for farmers as well as a symbol of wealth. A hog knocking at the door indicates wealth will come. In the picture two hogs hold gold in their mouths and carry gold on their backs and they are knocking at the door with luck. They are followed by pearls and treasure. A money tree grows in the courtyard, under which lies a treasure bowl. On both sides hang symbols of a perpetual source of wealth. The inscriptions on the treasure bowl point out the theme—wishes for prosperity.

Higher and Higher

In this picture a treasure bowl lies below containing various treasures on which stand five moppets which are standing higher and higher one by one. The five moppets lift, carry and hold fish, peaches and S-shaped sceptres, symbolizing abundance and long life. "Higher and Higher" are inscribed on the treasure bowl. All these signs show a clear wish.

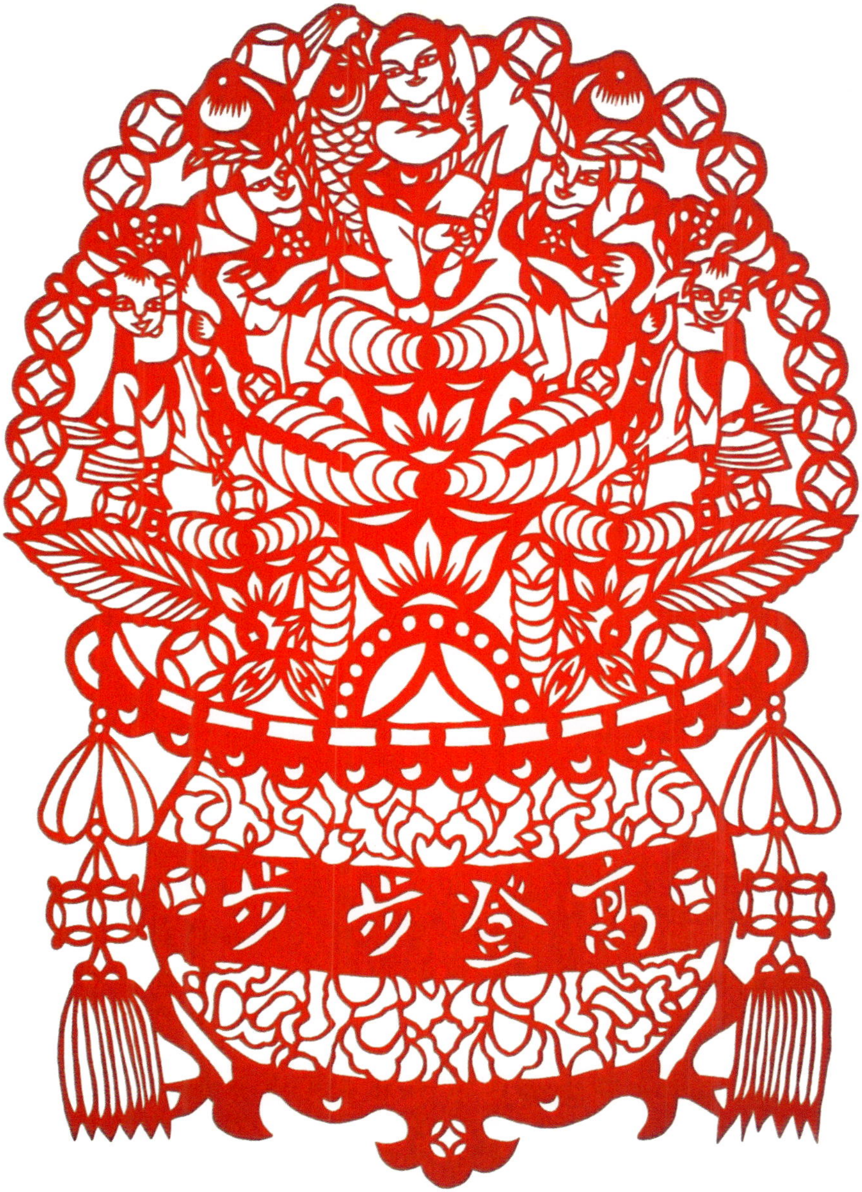

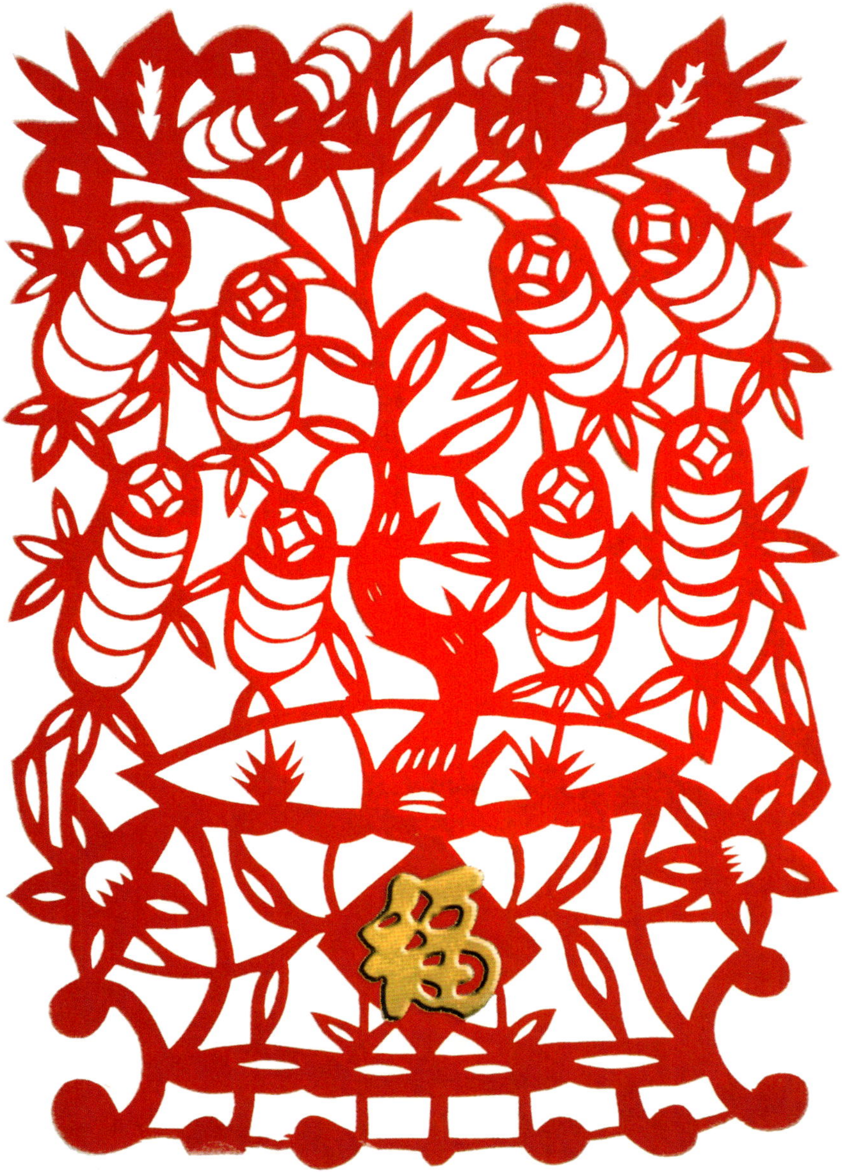

The Money Tree

This is a money tree and next to it is a treasure bowl. For those "lucky designs and words" it is wrong to regard them only as wishes for gaining money. A folk saying goes like this, "Man is a prong for making money and woman is a box for saving money." It refers to hardworking and thrift. Hardworking is the money tree and thrift is the treasure bowl.

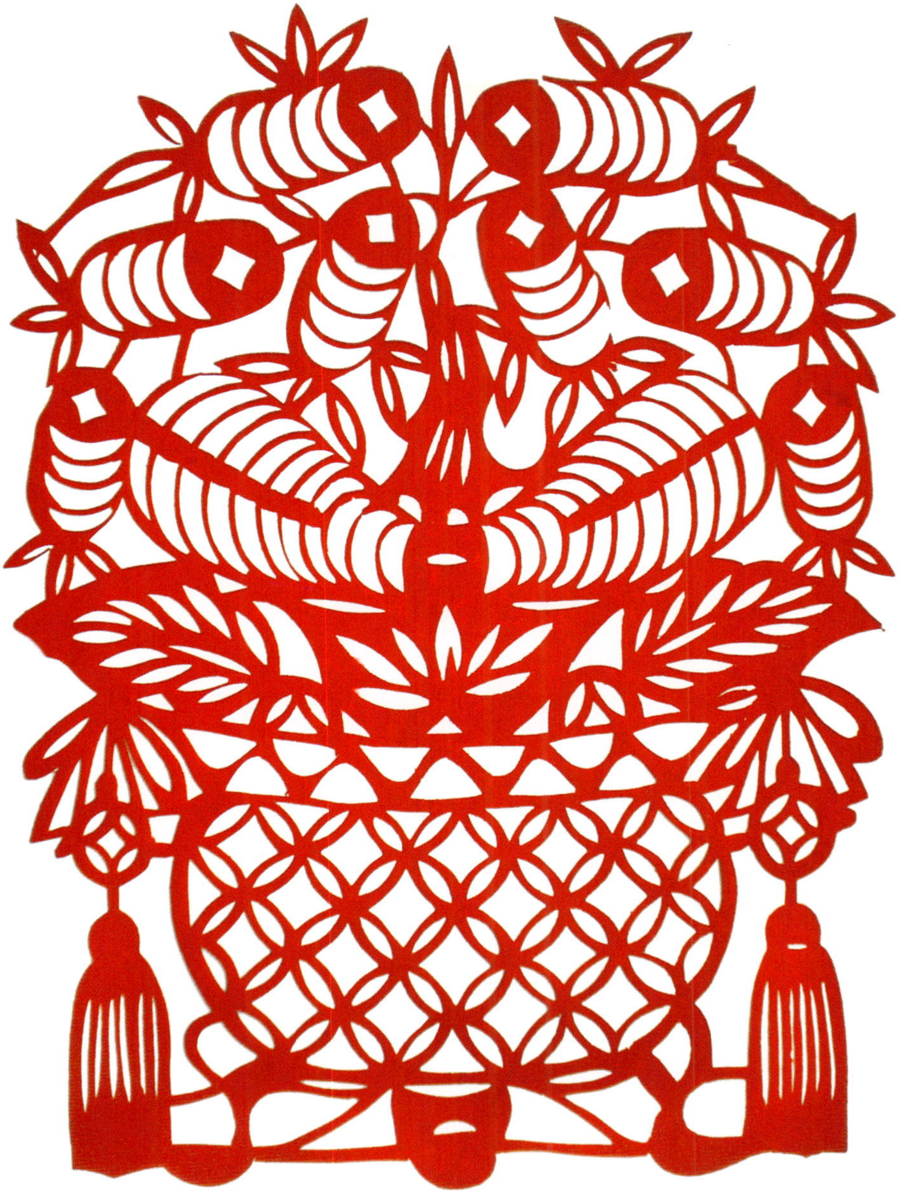

A Treasure Bowl
(ibid)

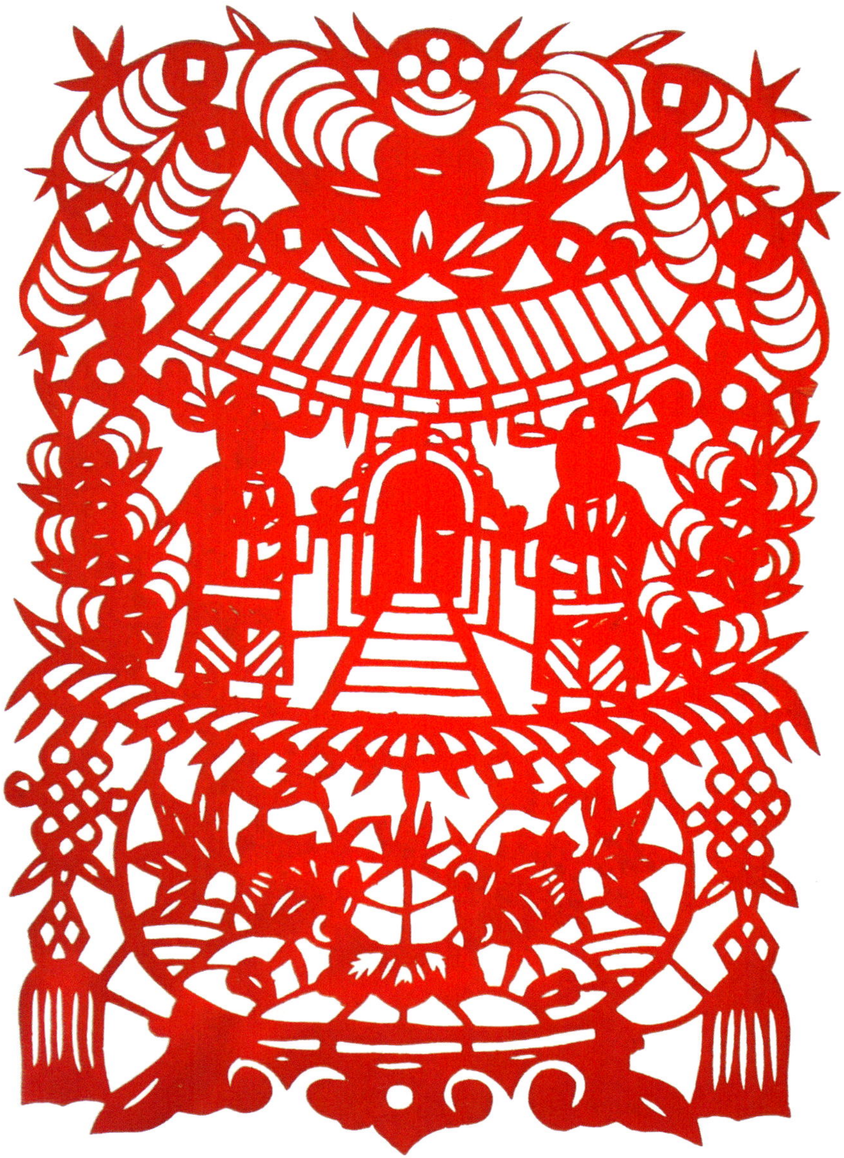

A Hall Packed with Riches

In this picture shoe-shaped gold and money above symbolize gold. The two fish symbolize jade and the two friends in the middle "fill the hall." According to Chinese traditional culture, gold is the most precious among all the metals. Jade is the most valuable among stones, gentle outside but firm inside with good virtue and character. Hence, pure and upright people are regarded as having a heart of gold and men of honour can compete with jade in terms of virtue. As a whole, it has the meaning that "upright and high-minded people gather in a hall."

Category of Pictures for a Wedding

Paper-cuts are also pasted on and put in the bridal chamber. People regard weddings and pregnancy as great happy events. These papercuts are mostly made and arranged in the room by the sisters-in-law or aunt of the new couple. They commonly use techniques of partial tones and metaphor to narrate matters related to sexual life and give the new couple some sex education.

For example, take the large ball of flowers pasted in the middle of the ceiling of the bridal chamber. In the centre is a round pattern of two fish mating. Fish in Chinese folklore, not only symbolizes abundance, but also carries the meaning of many offspring because it has an extremely large number of eggs. In the circumference lies a symbol of continuation. Hence, the meaning in it is clear. Designs around it include a boy and a girl talking love in front of peonies. On the ragged edge is a circle of designs symbolizing everything goes well. There is something very clear in the picture which is difficult to say here. Also there are pictures such as a "snake circling a rabbit," an "eagle chasing a rabbit," a "rooster bringing a child," "fish amusing themselves among the lotus" and "lotus giving birth to child" which show directly the relationship between sexual life and pregnancy and child bearing.

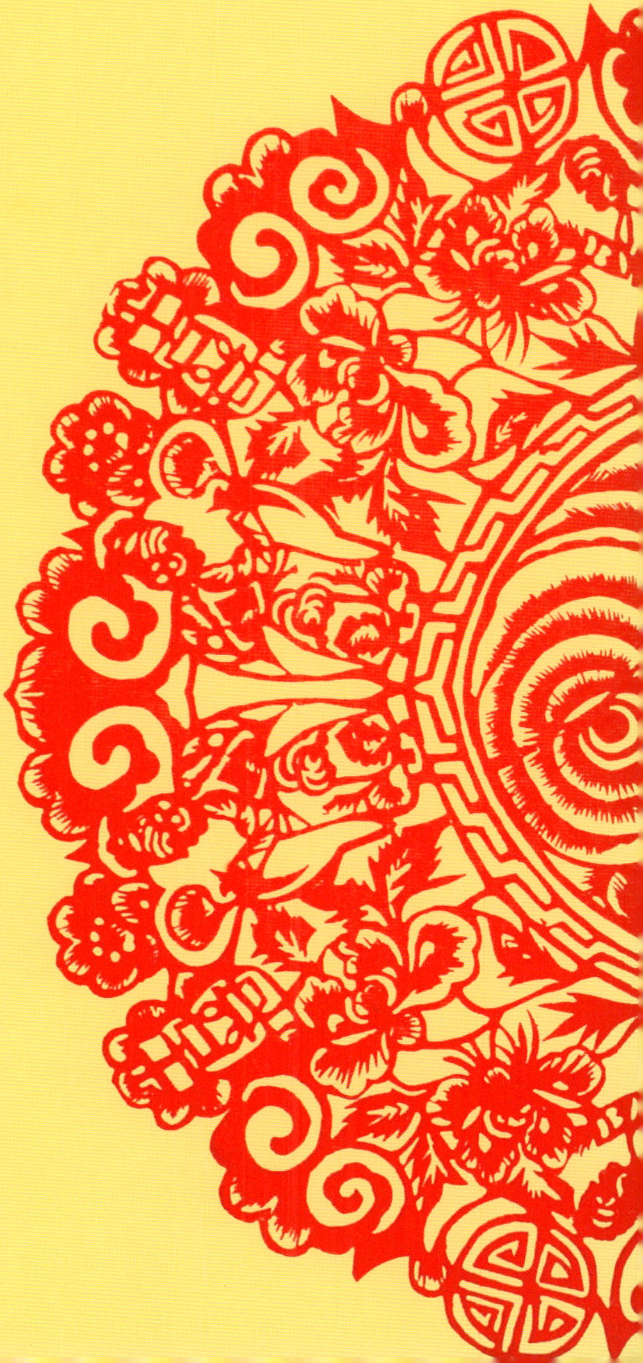

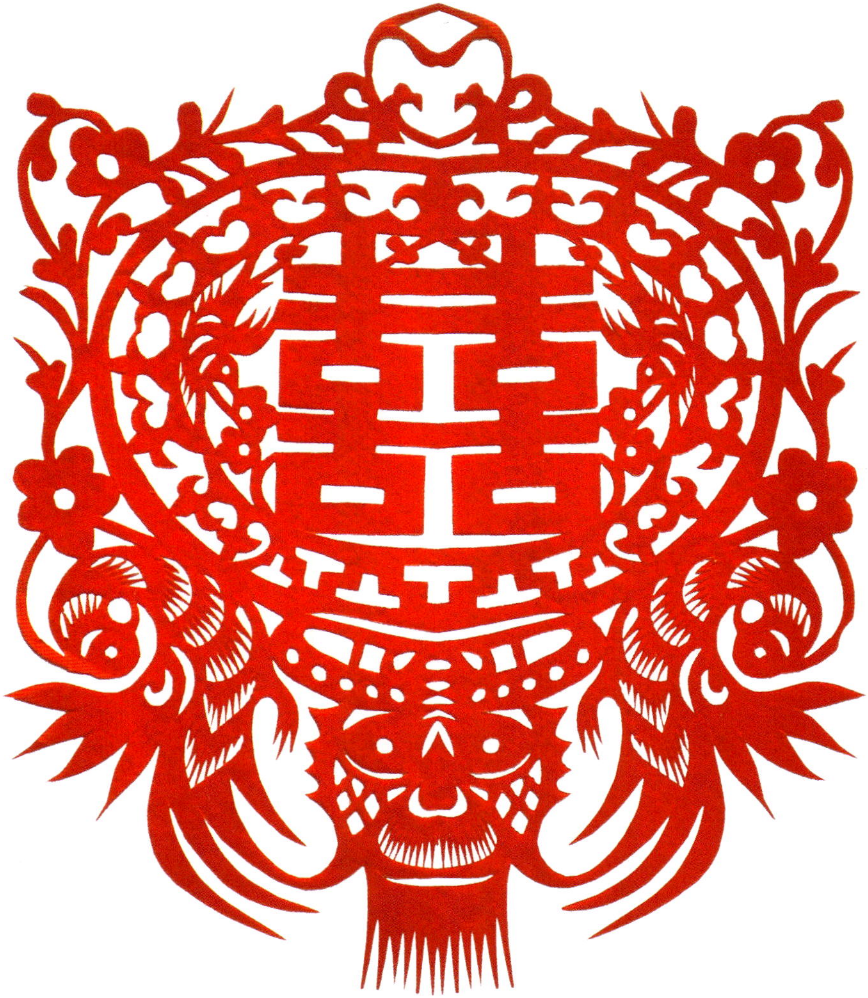

Special for Bridal Chamber

Chinese word " 喜 " (*Xi*) (meaning "happiness") is used for happy occasions, such as wedding. Very often, two " 喜 " (*Xi*) are put together to court double happiness and this is indispensable for bridal chambers.

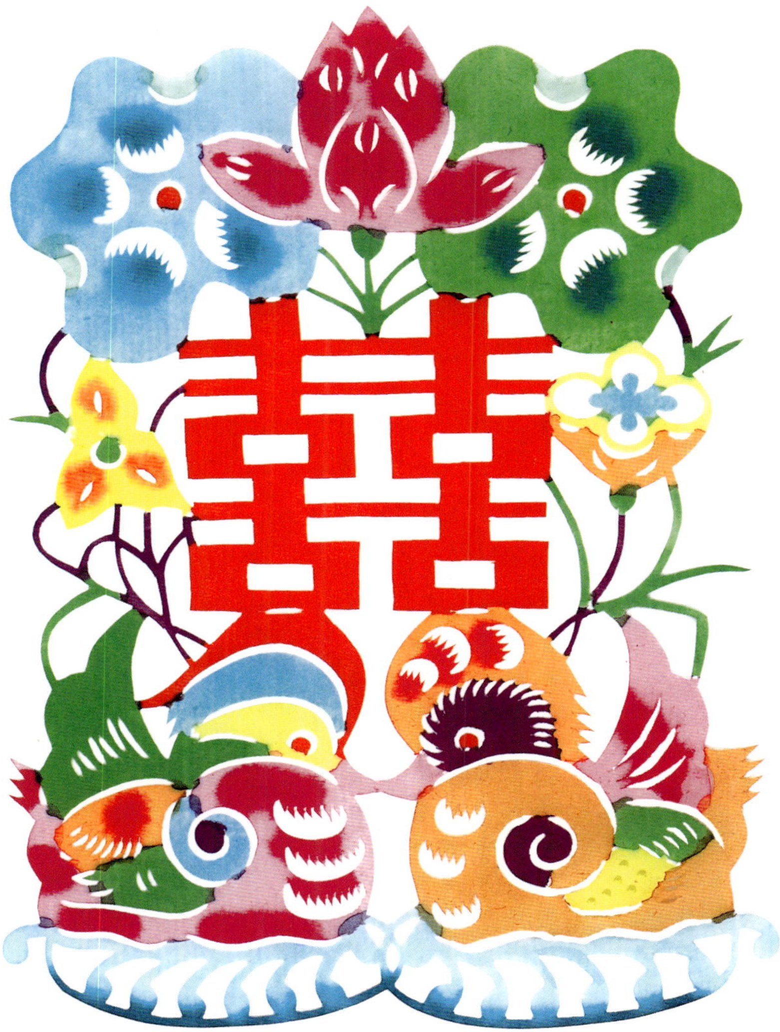

Double-Happiness Mandarin Ducks

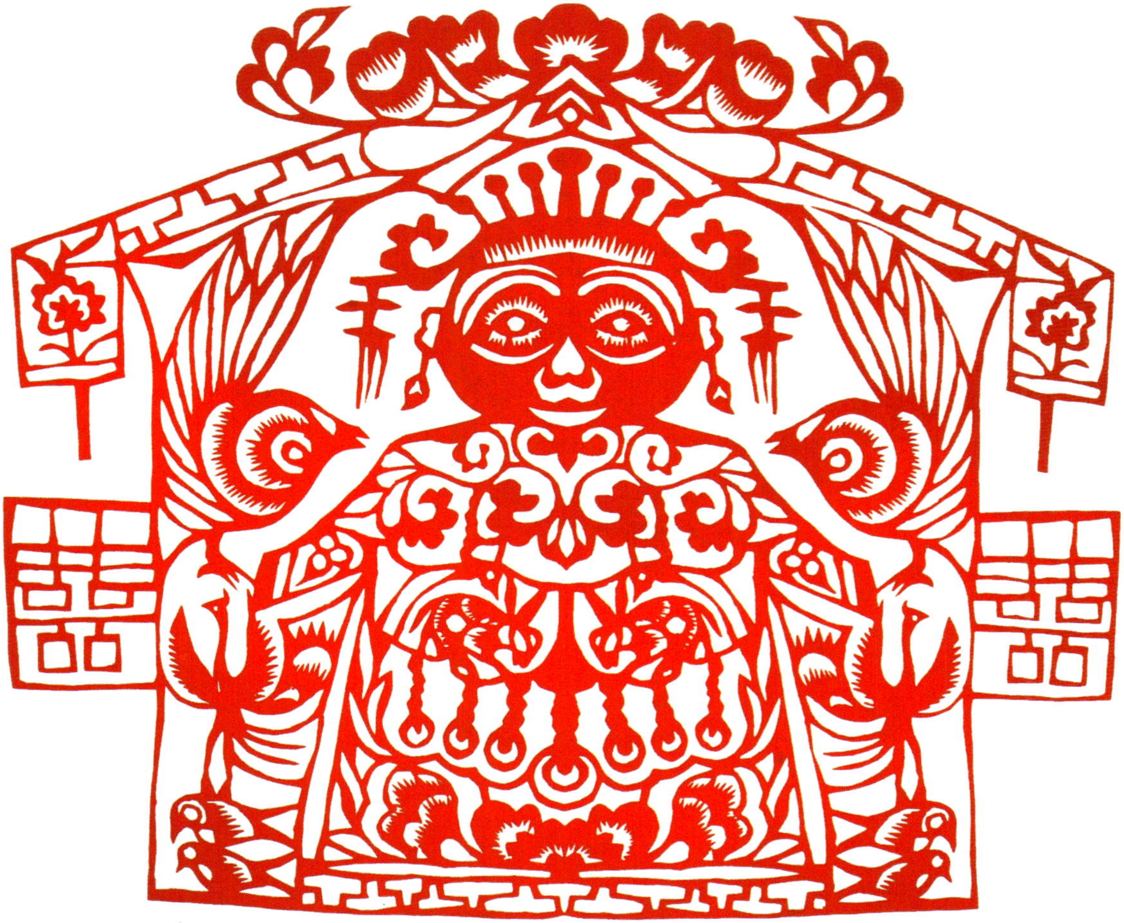

Special for Bridal Chamber

When the bridal sedan chair carries a girl to her husband's family, her life as a girl ends and her marriage begins. In this picture the two hands of the girl are replaced by two male birds which signifiy the combination of *yin* and *yang*. The design of an "eagle chasing a rabbit" on the front of the girl's chest and that of "two swallows mating" at the bottom corners on both sides imply the wish for the couple to have a happy life.

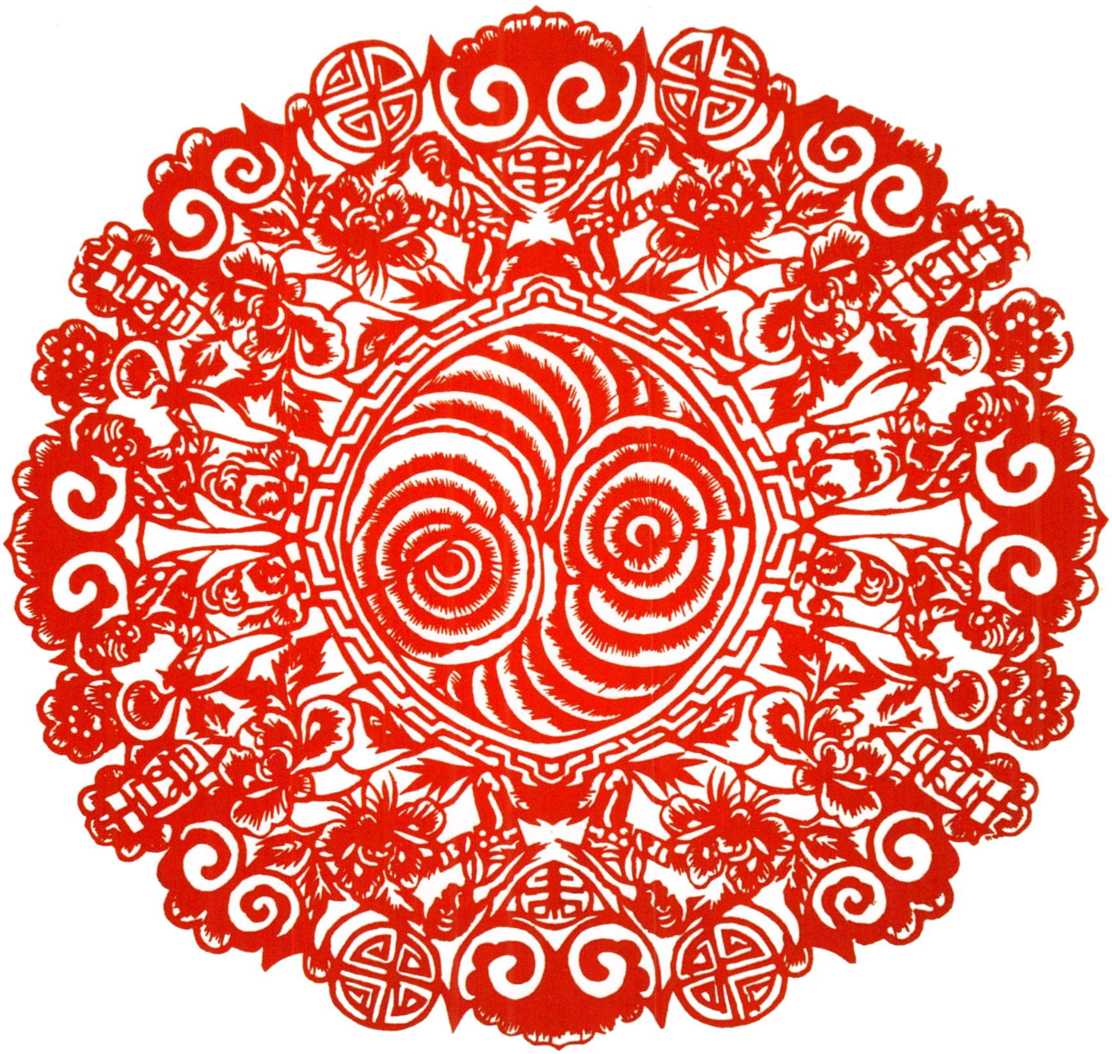

Special for Bridal Chamber

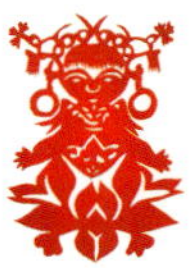

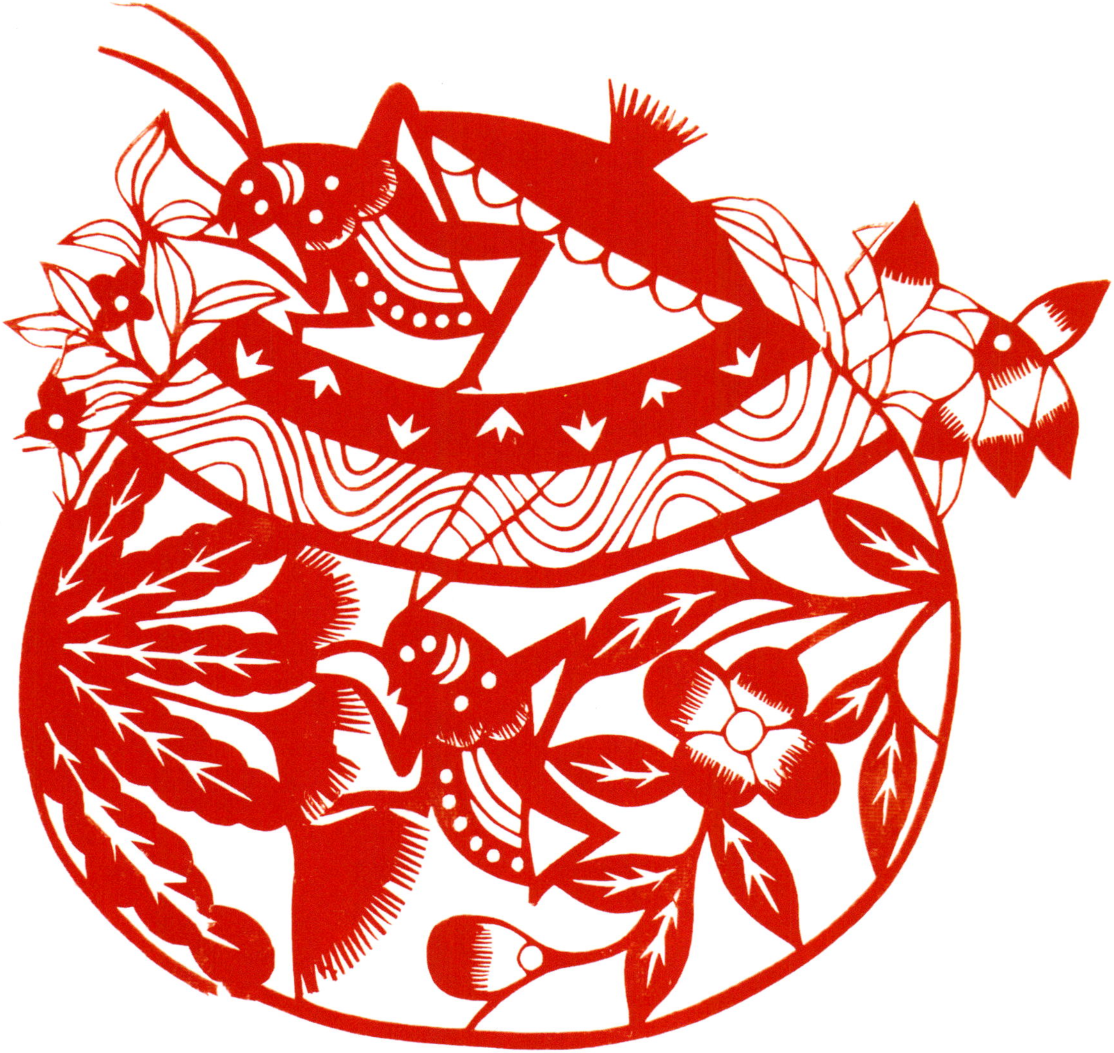

Special for Bridal Chamber

The cricket sings just like calling a brother. Pasting a paper-cut in the shape of a cricket shows the wish for having a boy.

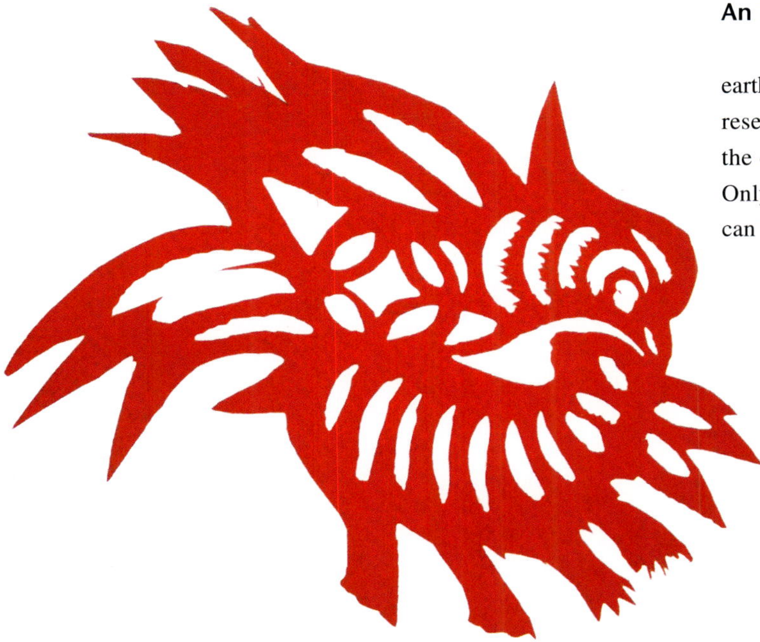

An Eagle Chasing a Rabbit

In Chinese folklore heaven is masculine and earth female. As the eagle flies in the sky it represents the masculine side. The rabbit runs on the earth and so it represents the female side. Only copulation between a man and a woman can bring a child into being.

A Snake Circling a Rabbit

Small-scale peasant economy has existed in China for several thousand years. For the prosperity of the family parents hoped their sons would marry early and have children. Hence, boys in rural areas would get married at the age of 15 or 16. In fact they were nothing more than big boys, so a comparatively mature wife two years older than them was needed. First, she could help do housework; second, she could take care of the young husband. A girl who was born in the Year of the Rabbit is older than the boy who was born in the Year of Snake. Hence, a folk saying goes like this, " If a snake circles a rabbit the family will surely be rich." Therefore, making a paper cut in the shape of "a snake circling a rabbit" to paste in the bridal chamber speaks louder than words.

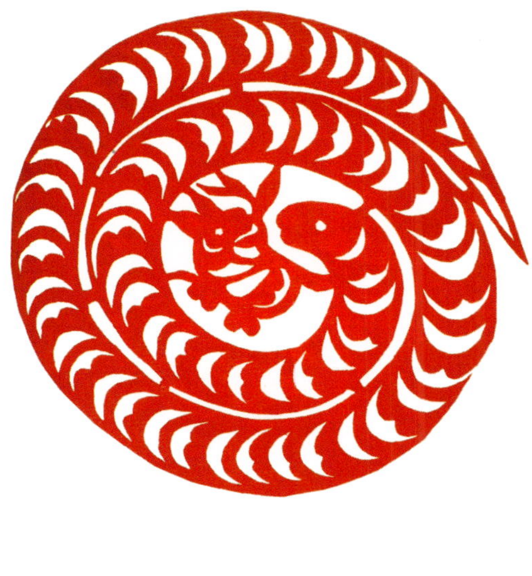

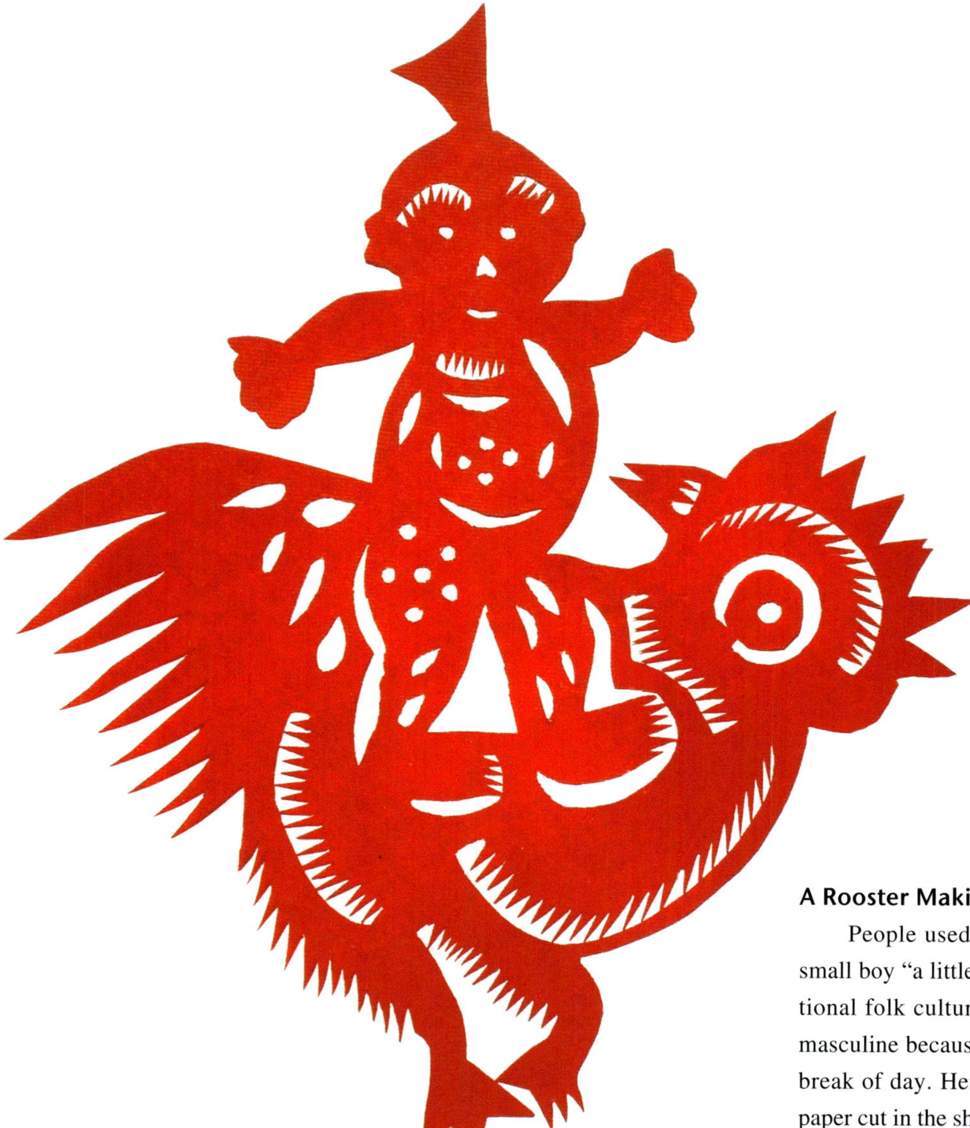

A Rooster Making a Child

People used to call the penis of a small boy "a little cock." Chinese traditional folk culture regards the cock as masculine because the cock heralds the break of day. Hence, the meaning of a paper cut in the shape of "a rooster making a child" and pasting it in the bridal chamber is clear.

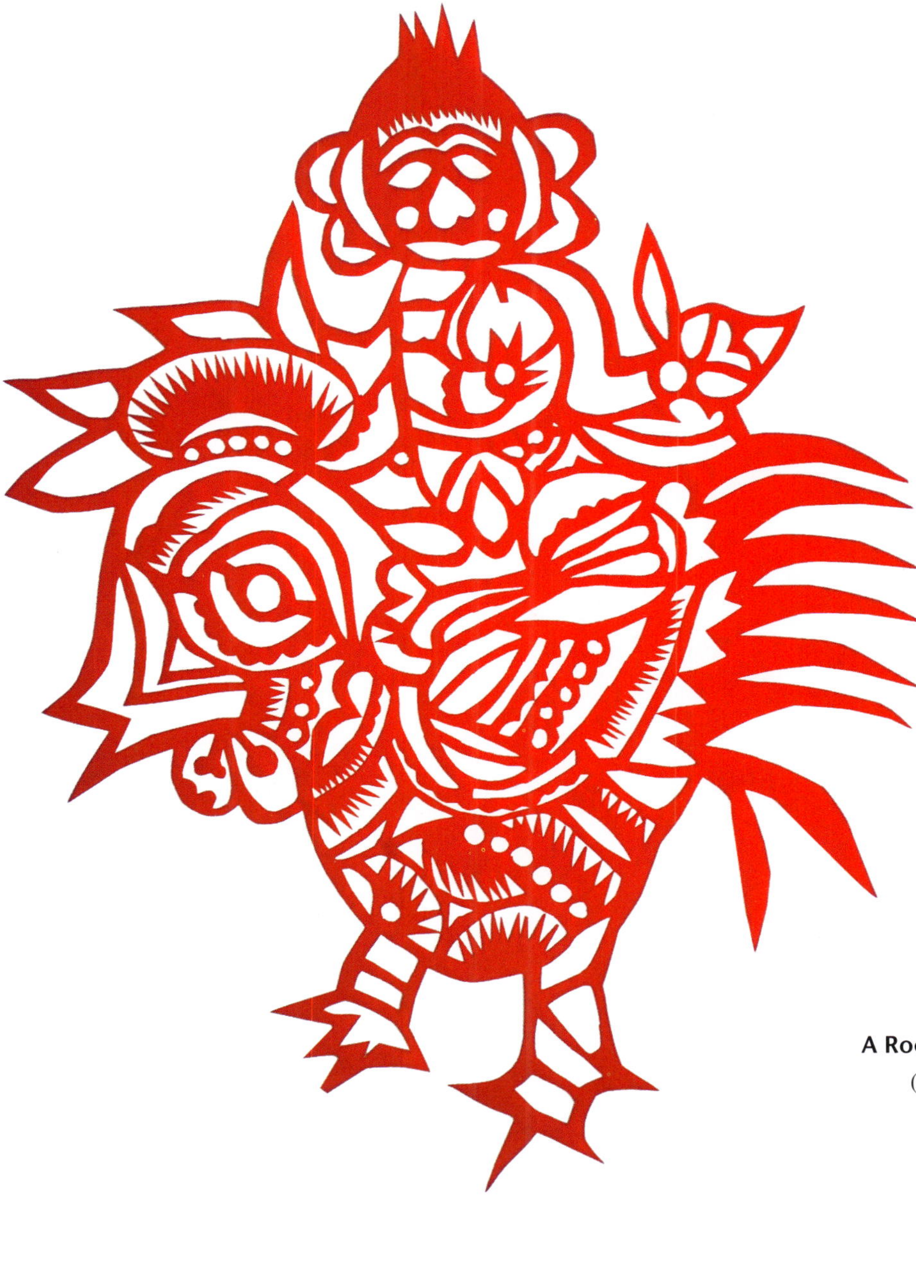

A Rooster Making a Child
(ibid)

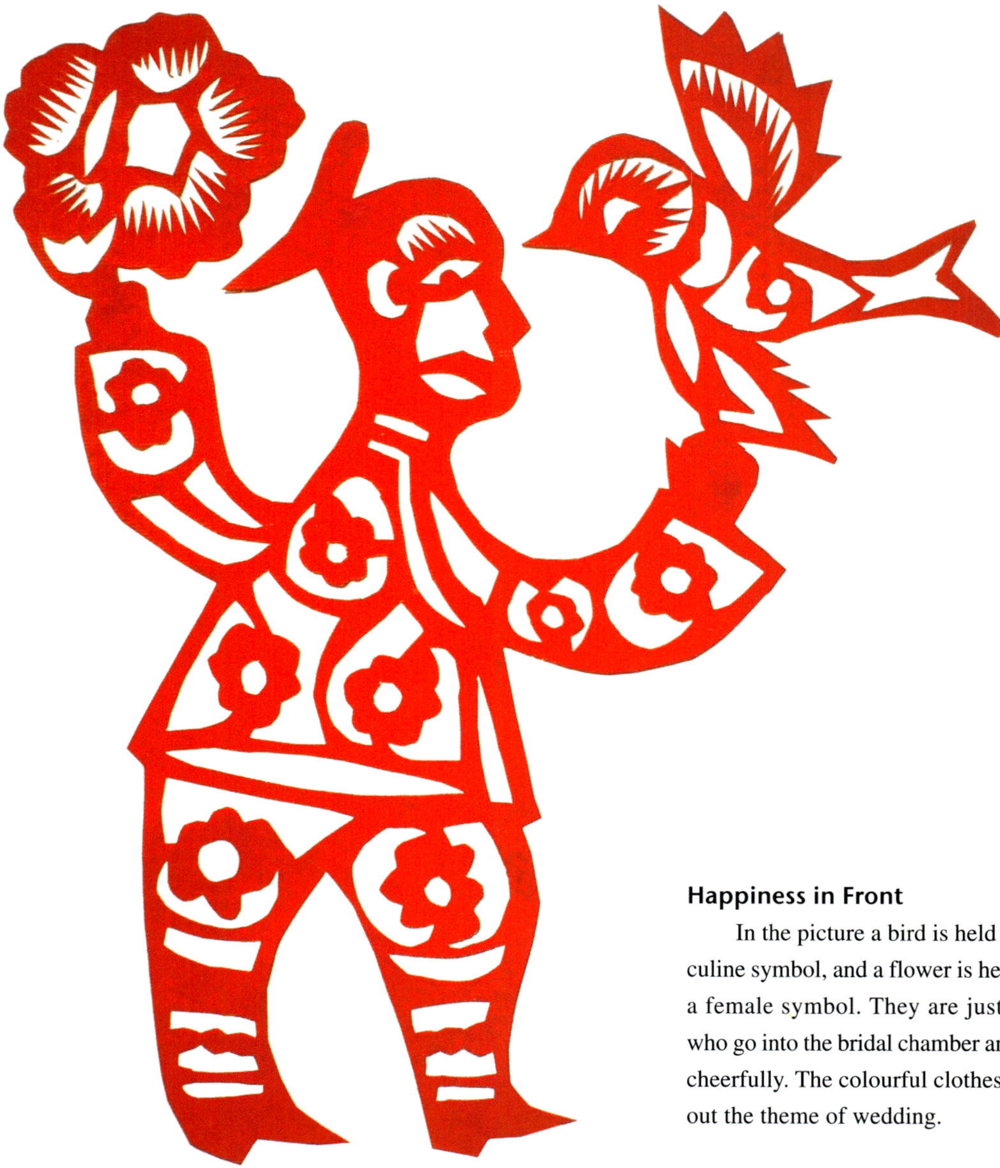

Happiness in Front

In the picture a bird is held in one hand, a masculine symbol, and a flower is held in the other hand, a female symbol. They are just like a new couple who go into the bridal chamber and look at each other cheerfully. The colourful clothes of the person point out the theme of wedding.

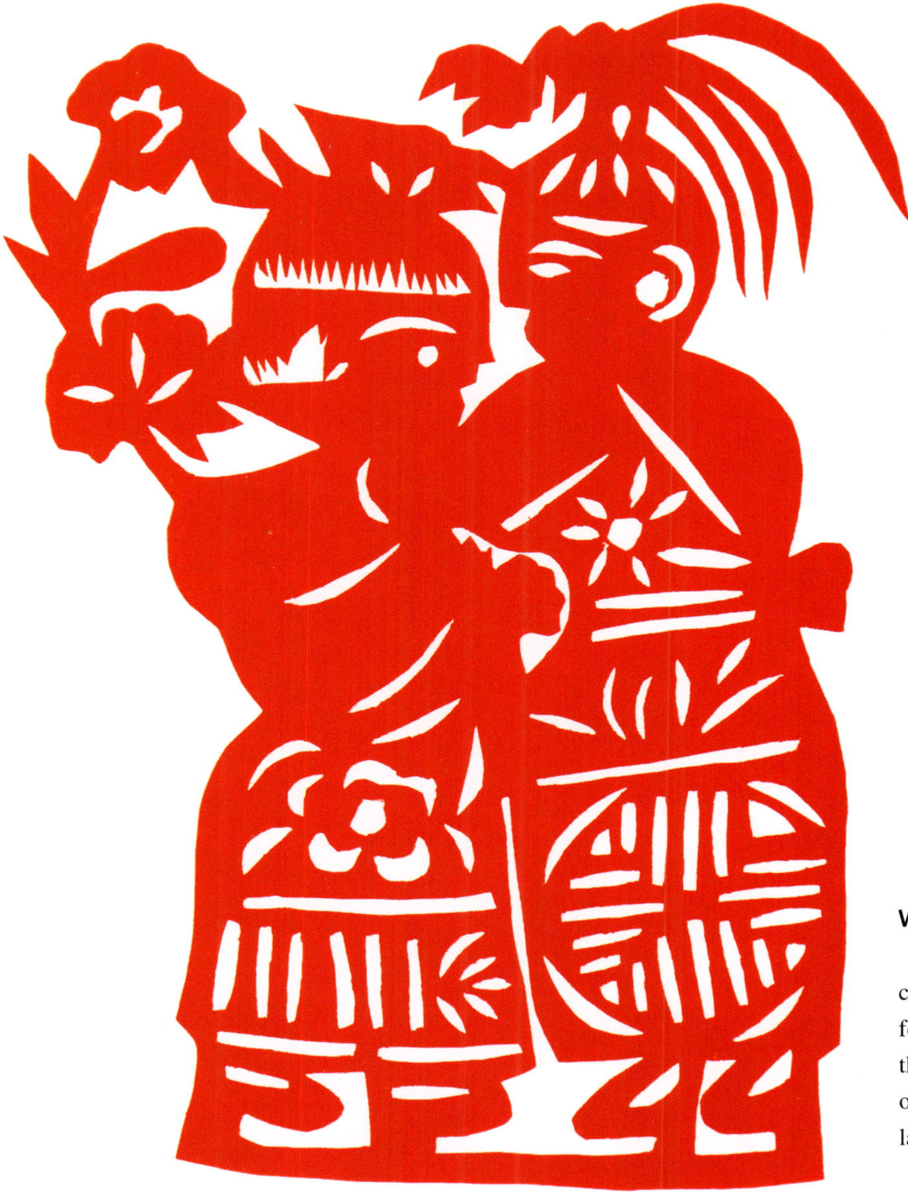

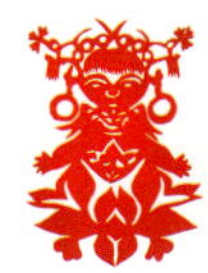

Wedding Ceremony

In the picture the new couple embrace each other. The female is holding a peony and the man is carrying a phoenix on his head. Its meaning is similar "Happiness in Front."

Bearing a Child

In the picture a child sits on a pair of egg-shaped objects which, as a whole, look like the penis. In order to make the new couple see clearly, the legs of the child are cut into the shape of a penis and a design of copulation lies in the middle of the two egg-shaped objects.

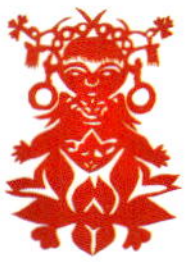

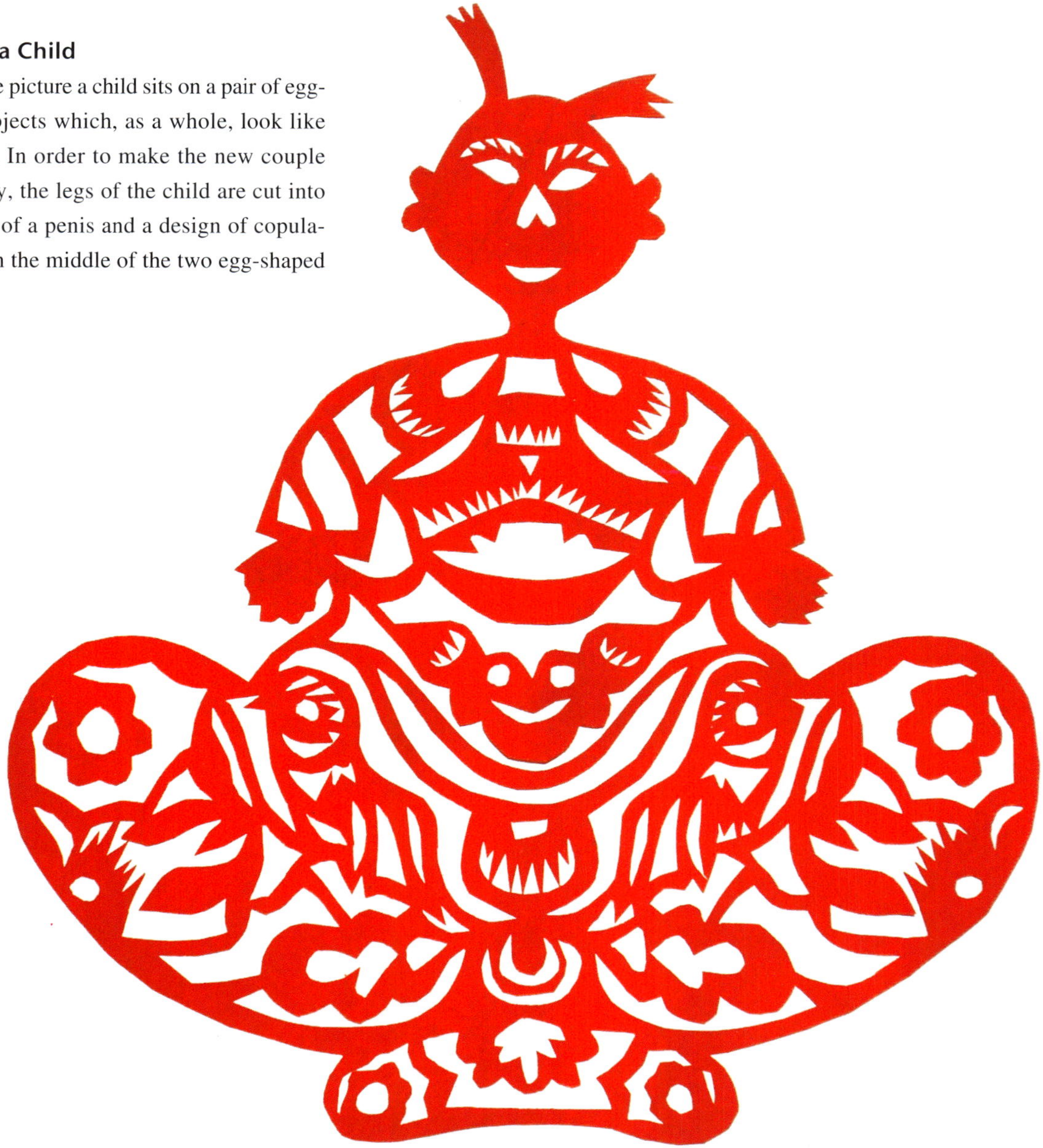

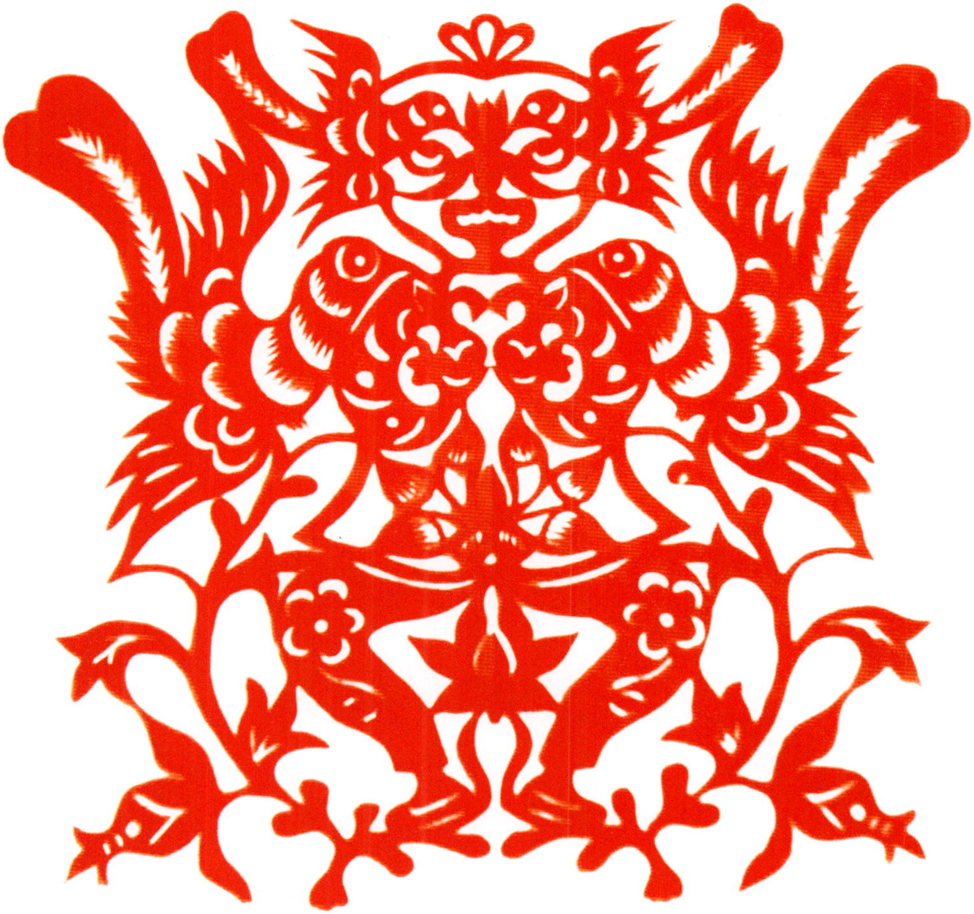

Happiness on the Eyebrows

In the picture the two eyebrows of the person are cut into a pair of flying magpies as are the arms, which add a festive atmosphere to it. The key point is that it is a masculine symbol. Under his crotch lie lotus flowers which symbolize a female. As a whole, it is a picture depicting copulation between a man and a woman. The guava and lotus flowers have the meaning of giving birth to child.

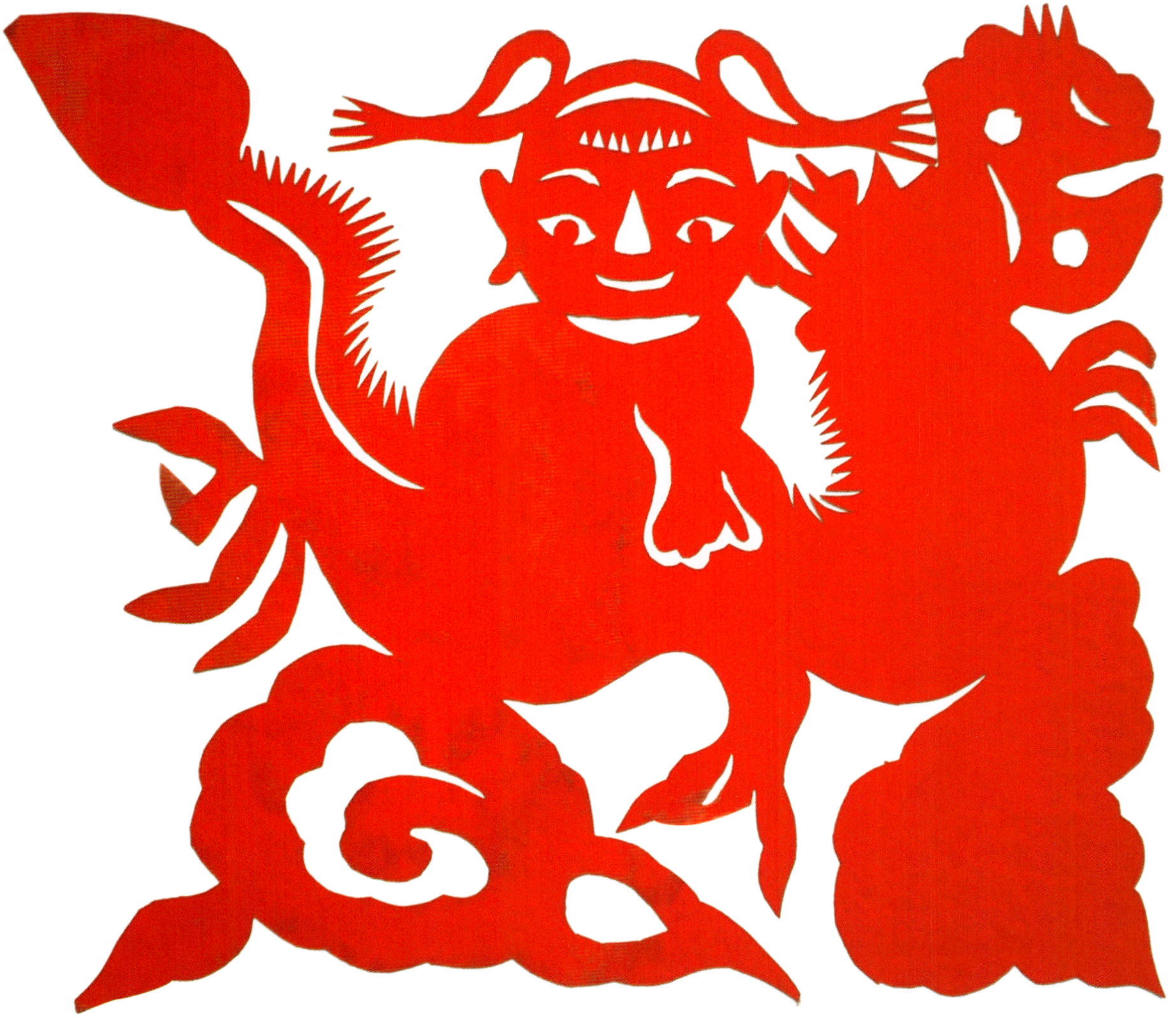

Dragon Brings a Child

It is to bless the new couple to have a child at an earlier date.

A Lotus Flower Bearing a Child

In the areas of Gansu, Shaanxi and Shanxi provinces such pictures as a "fish amusing a lotus," " a fish eating a lotus," "a child sitting on a lotus" and "a lotus bearing a child" are used to depict the sweet honeymoon of a new couple. The five in this group depict love and copulation.

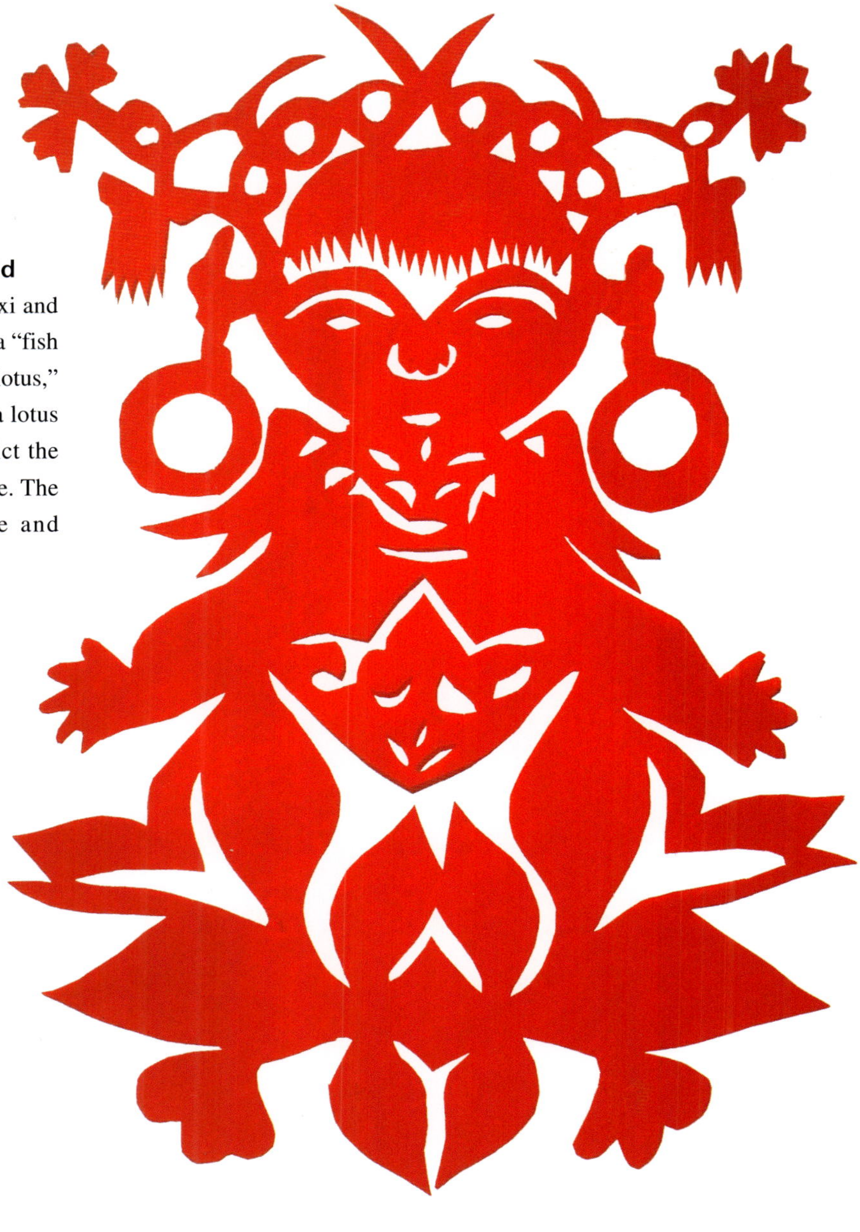

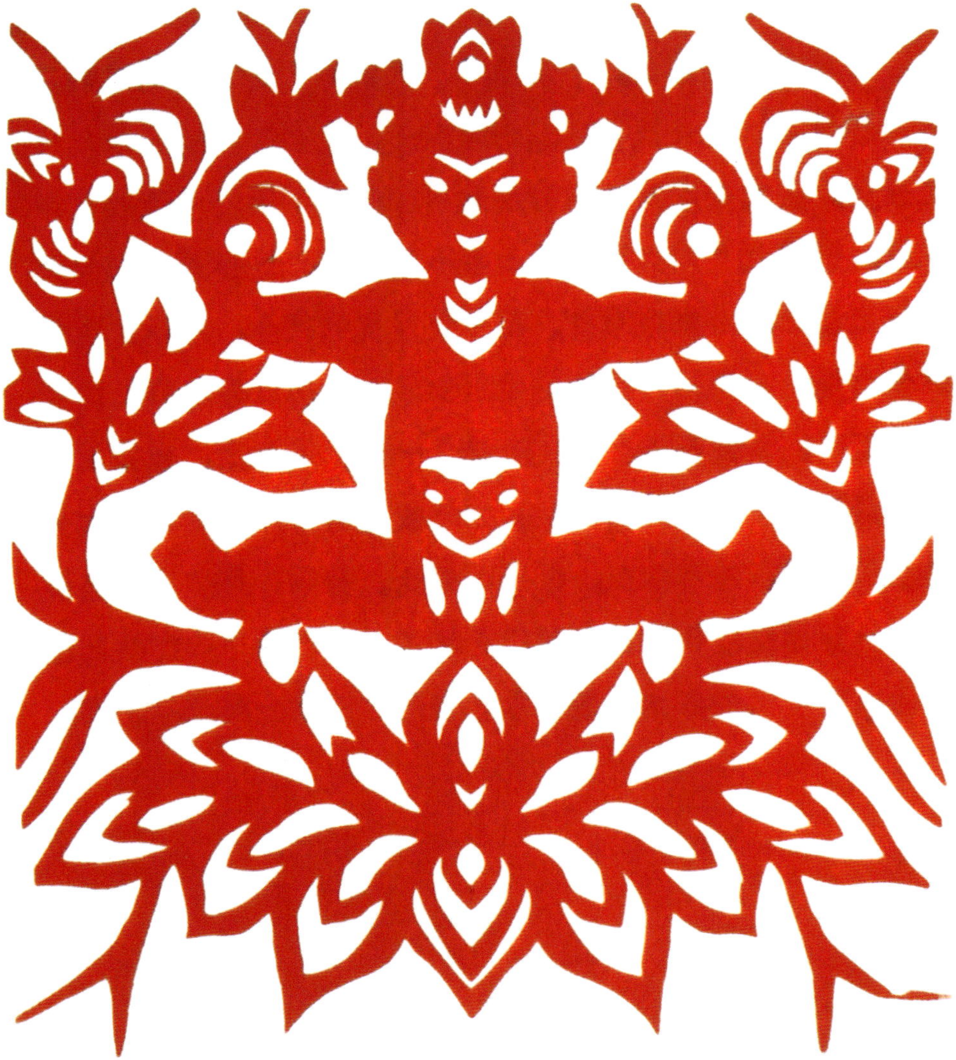

A Lotus Flower Bearing a Child

(ibid)

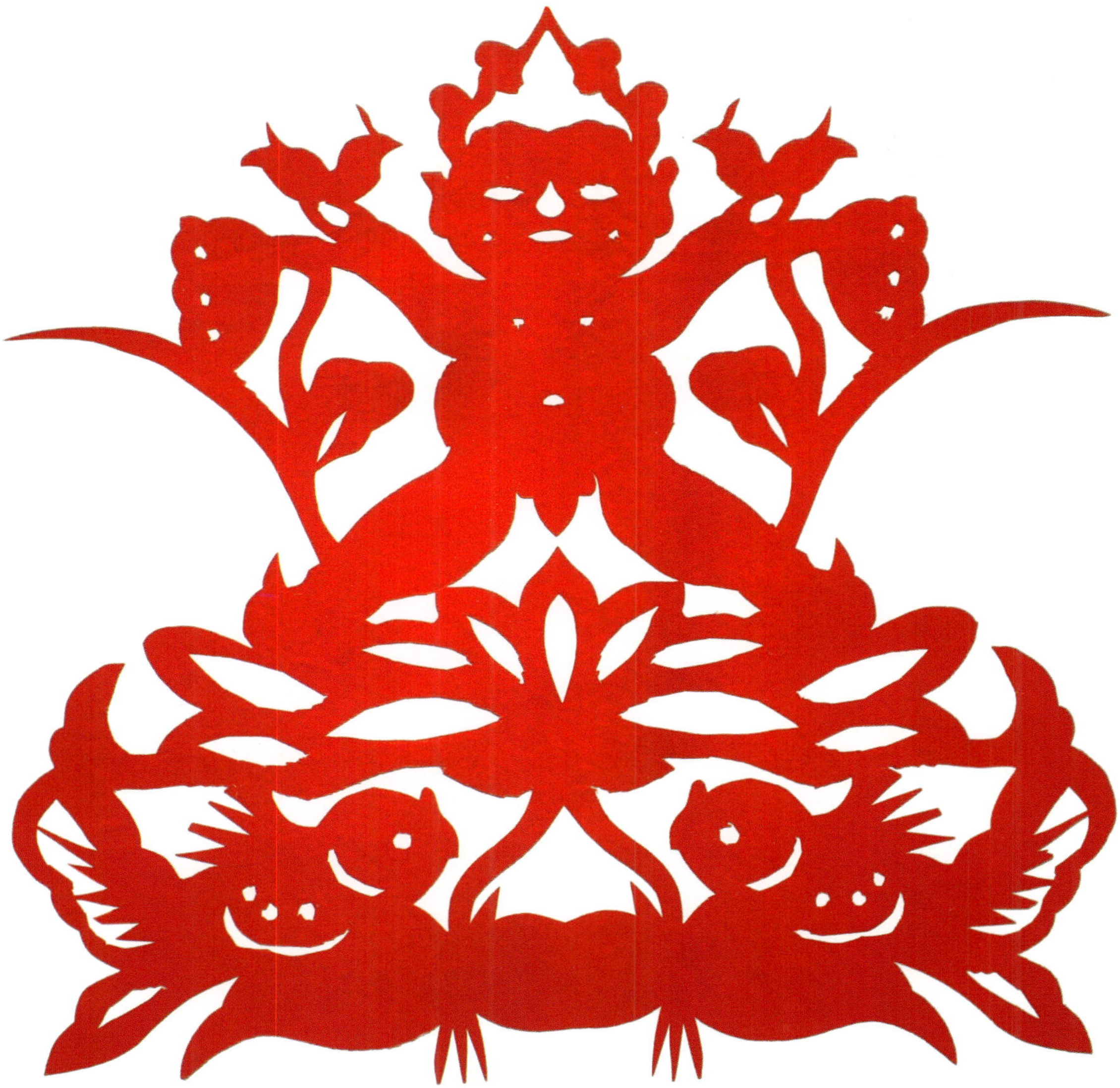

A Lotus Flower Bearing a Child
(ibid)

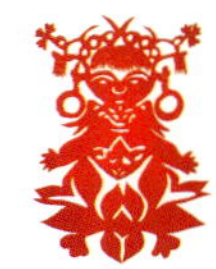

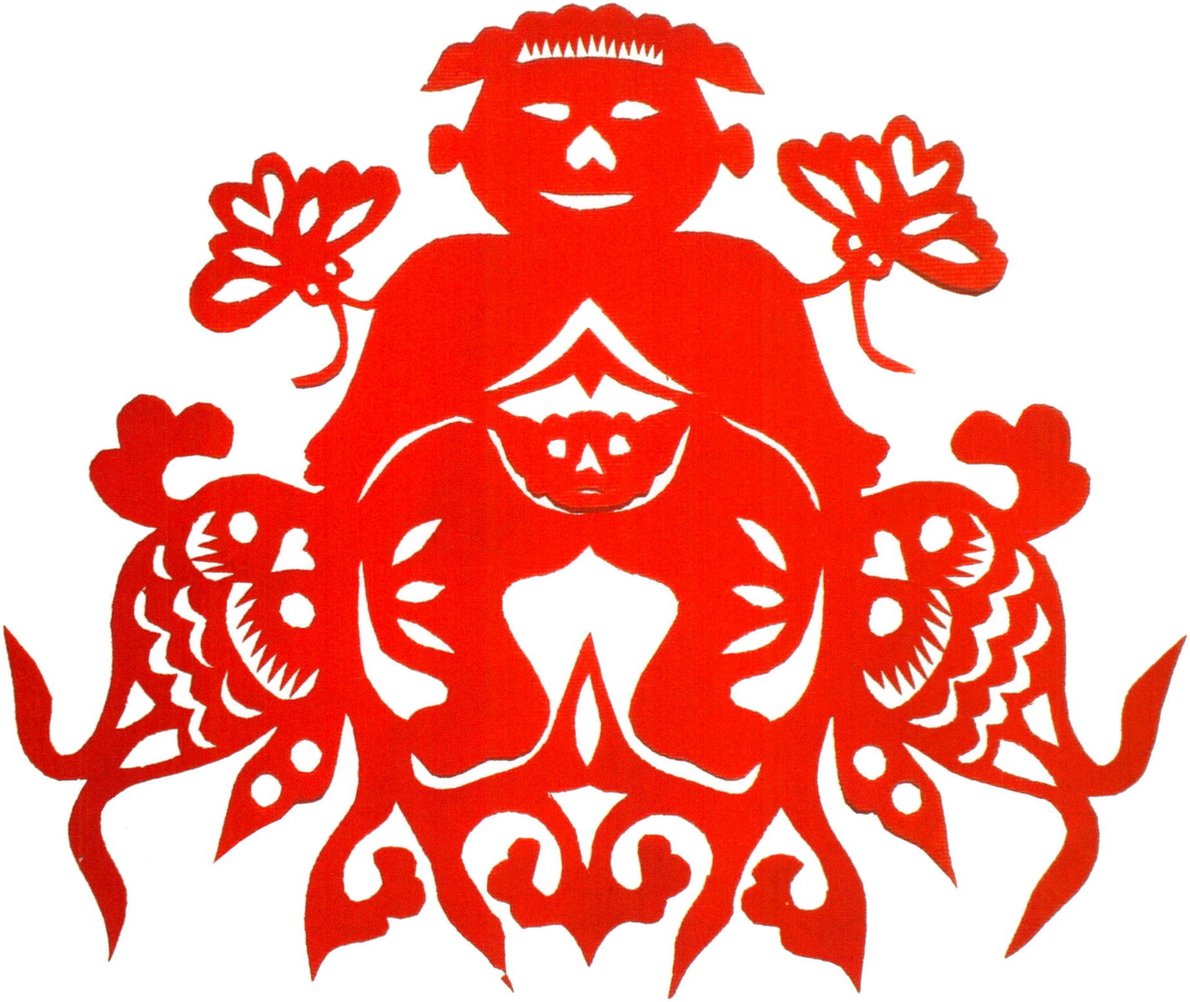

A Lotus Flower Bearing a Child
(ibid)

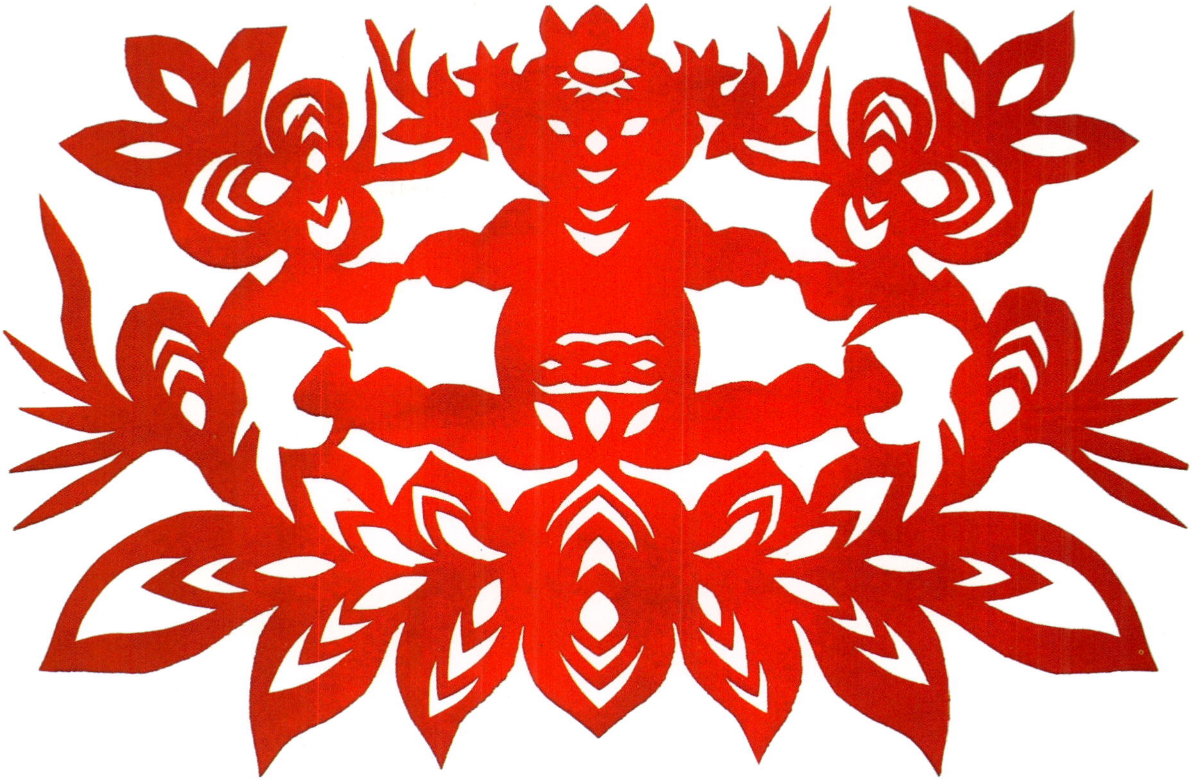

A Lotus Flower Bearing a Child

(ibid)

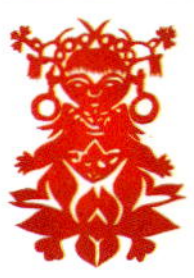

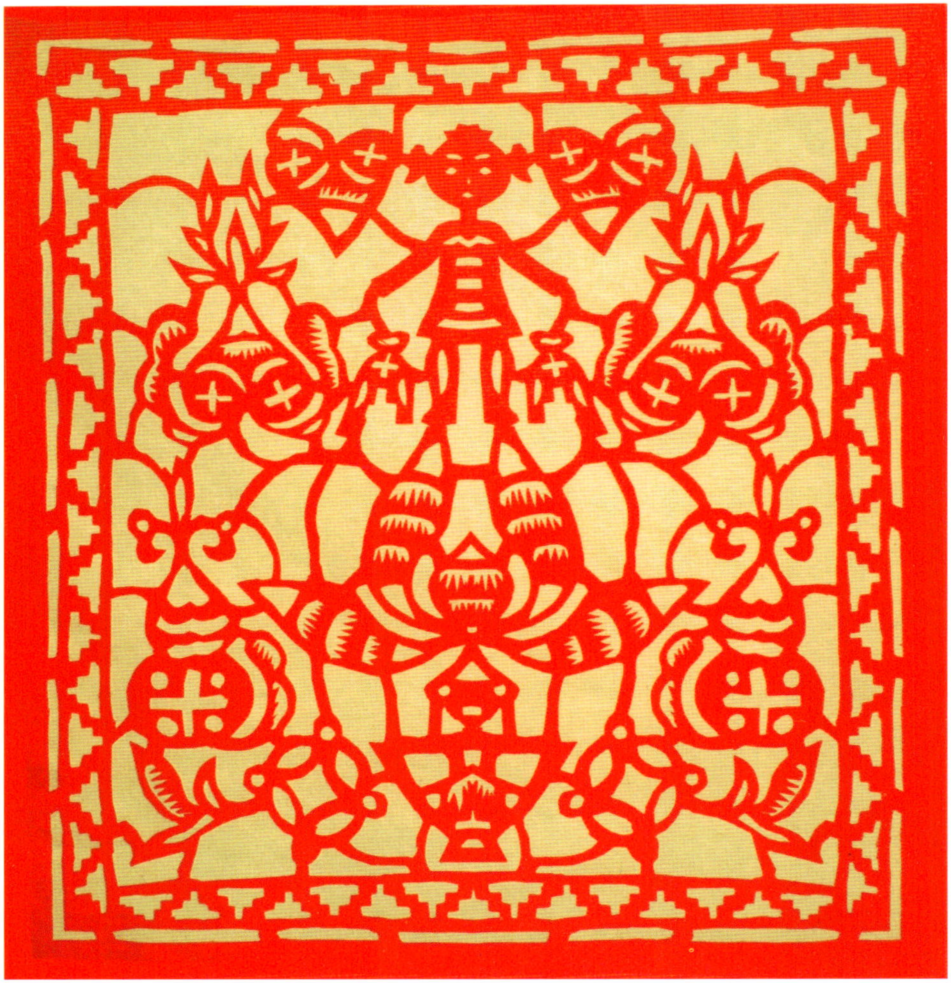

Wedding Chamber Decoration

This kind of "the Wedding Chamber Decoration" is similar to the picture of the two Chinese characters "*Xi,*" which are pasted on both sides of the door, in the hall and in the bridal chamber. It not only indicates the beginning of a new important life of the new couple, but also shows others' blessings for them, wishing them a harmonious life and wishing them to have a child early.

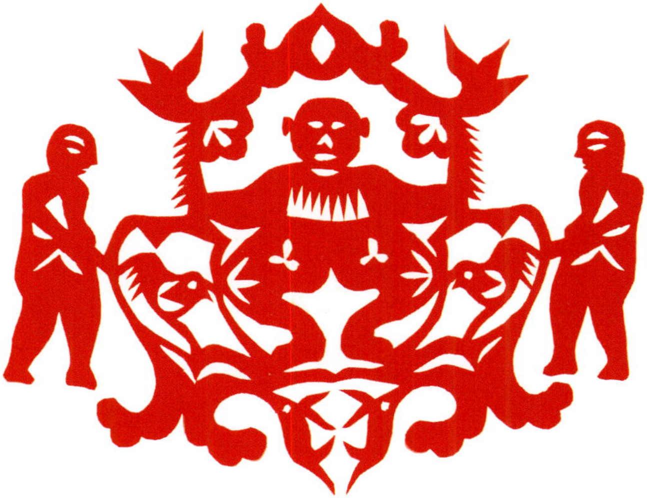

Wedding Chamber Decoration
(ibid)

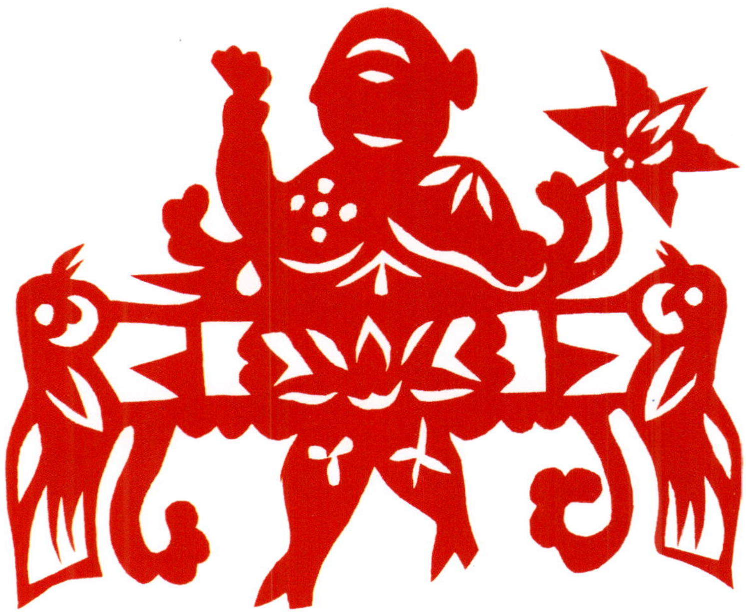

Wedding Chamber Decoration
(ibid)

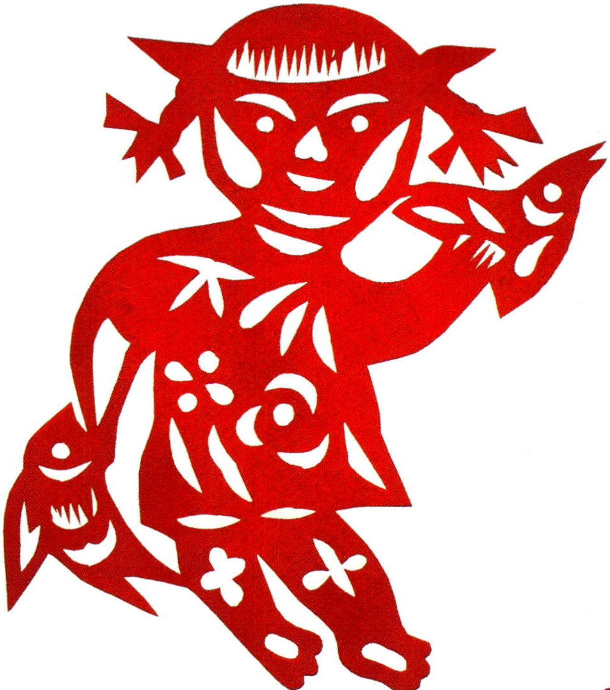

Cock-grasping Child

In the picture the girl has two hairpins on her head indicating that the girl has grown up. She holds two birds (masculine sign) in her hands with the meaning of copulation. This is a typical wedding picture.

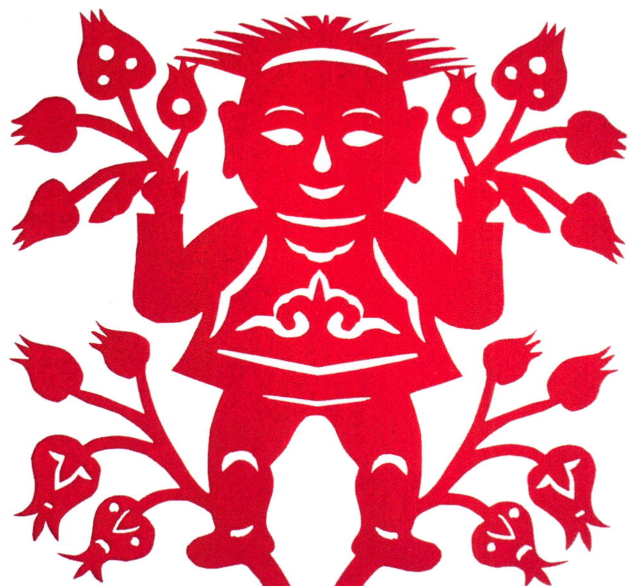

Pomegranate Full of Seeds

In Chinese, "seed" and "son" have the same pronounciation. This paper cut implies "many sons."

Category of Embroidery

China has always been a farming society and Chinese people have lived a one-household farming life for several thousand years. Men plough while women weave. Even a young boy is required to plough the farm and grow grain and cotton and a girl learn weaving, cutting and sewing at the age of eight or nine. Of all the crafts they learn paper-cutting and embroidery are the most common and they need long-term training. Rural girls cut figures on paper with a scissors instead of painting.

It is very simple for them to cut out livestock figures or stories on paper as vivid as the ones painted by artists. As a result the patterns for their embroideries are mostly cut with scissor. All these paper-cuts will end up being covered over when the embroidery is finished.

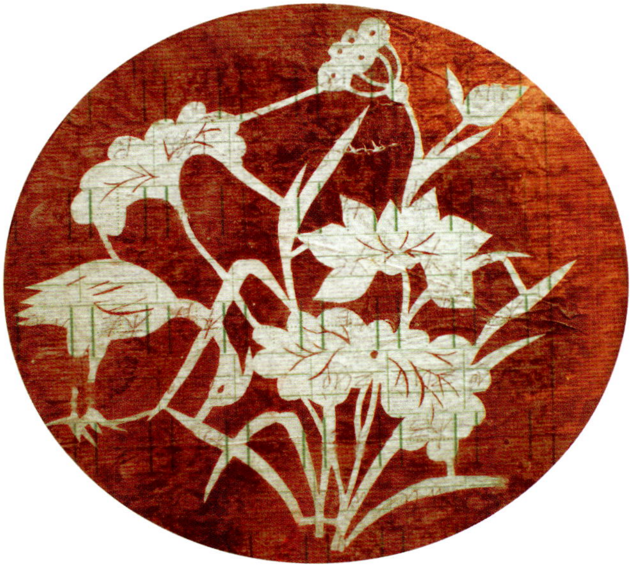

An Egret Lying on Lotus Flowers

It is a traditionally smoked paper-cut sample used as a master copy for an embroidered cover for a pillow. In the folk pictures the egret is compared to a male and the lotus flower a female. So the picture symbolizes copulation. This is true for new couples when they rest their heads on a pair of embroidered pillows. Embroidery art is blended with real life, naturally.

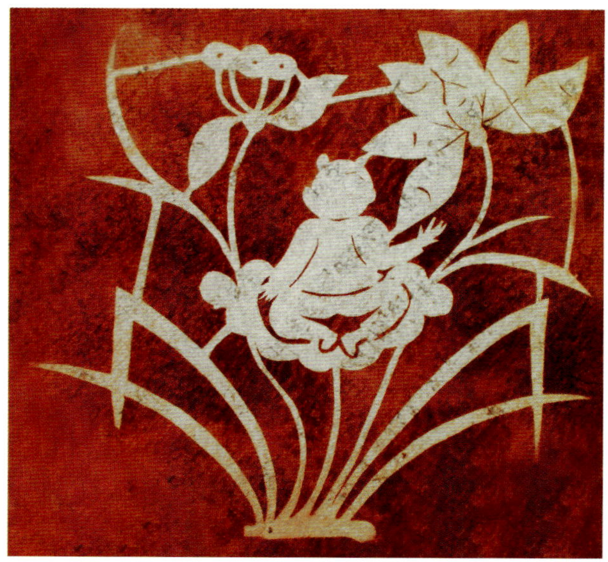

The Lotus Flower Giving Birth to Sons

The Lotus flower on the top right-hand side symbolizes a female and the one on the top left-hand side is in blossom and gives birth to sons. This implies that only copulation could bring a child. It is also a smoked paper-cut master copy for an embroidered cover for a pillow.

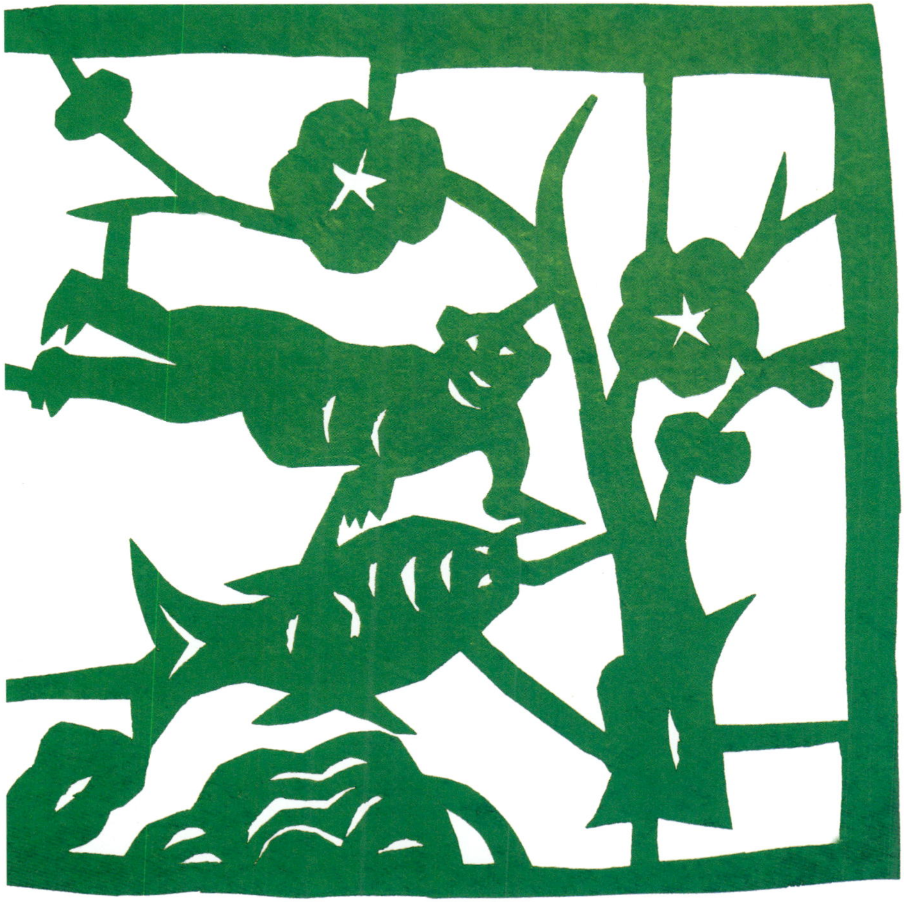

Wang Xiang Lying on the Ice Looking for Carp

Wang Xiang is one of the twenty-four filial examples. When he was a child his mother died and his stepmother was unloving toward him. During the cold winter when the river would be frozen, his stepmother liked to eat fresh fish. She would force him to go down to the river, where he had to take his clothes of and lie on the ice in order to melt it so that he could catch some carp. Suddenly the ice opened and a pair of carp leapt out. He caught them and returned to serve them to his stepmother. This style of embroidered pillow often reminds people of educating their children and serves as vivid teaching material.

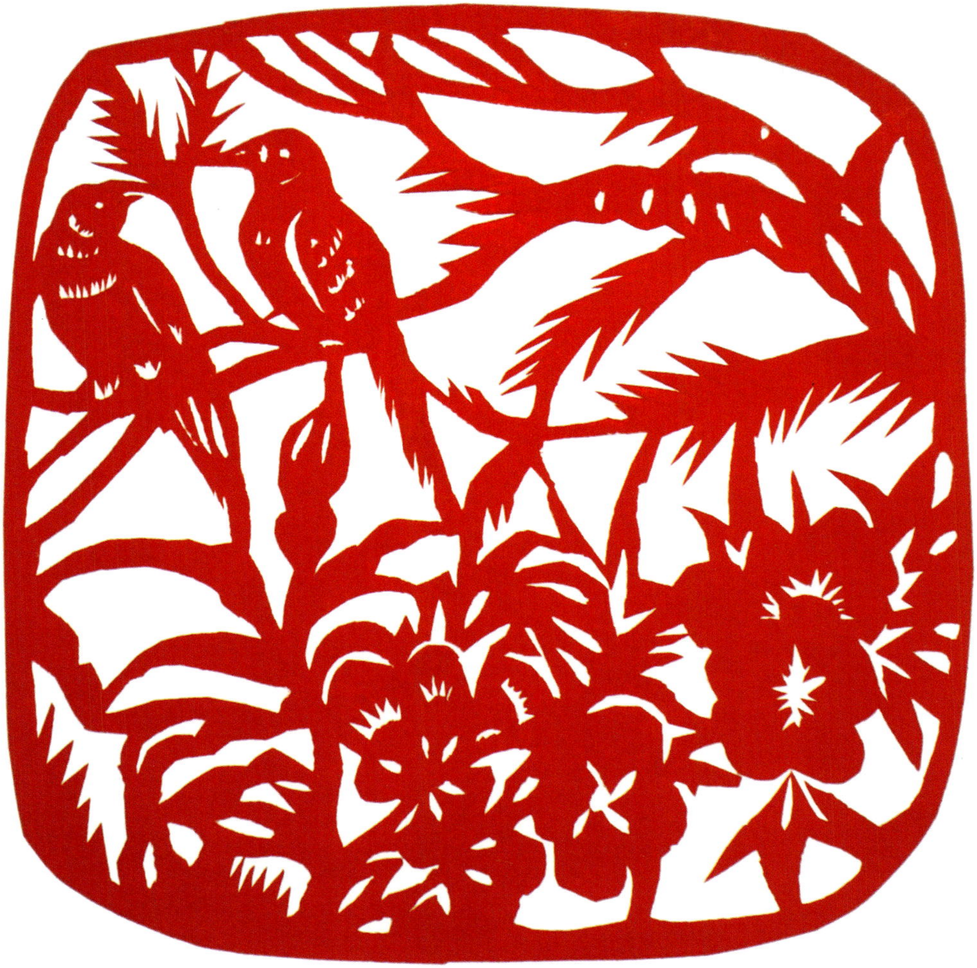

Double Magpies

Country people are very fond of the magpie because in the Chinese language the name of the magpie has the character of "*Xi* (happiness)." So people think that magpie can bring good things to them. Embroidering two magpies on a pillow implies that the new couple will never abandon each other.

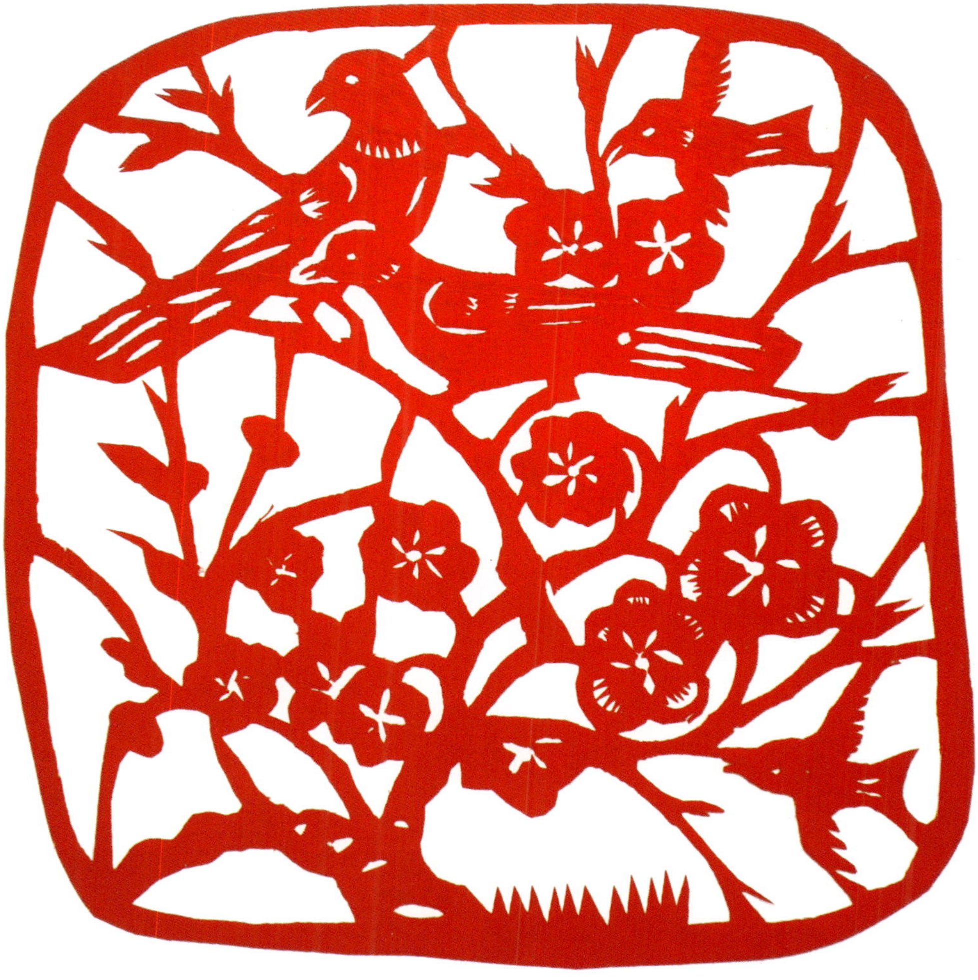

Birds Resting on a Plum Tree

Such titles as "birds resting on a plum tree," "birds playing on a plum tree" and "birds standing on plum trees" all have the meaning of a couple playing and copulating.

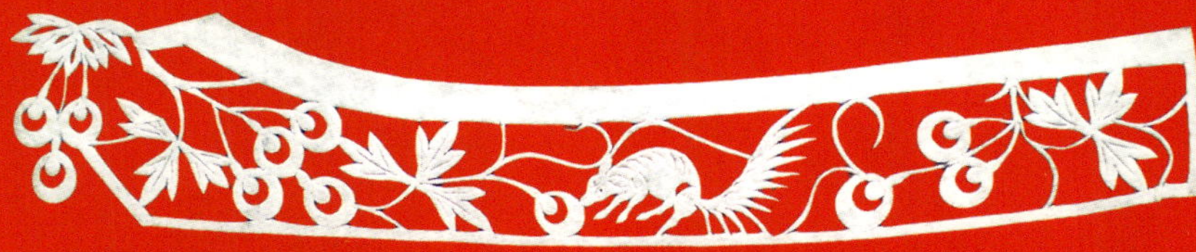

A Squirrel Stealing Grapes

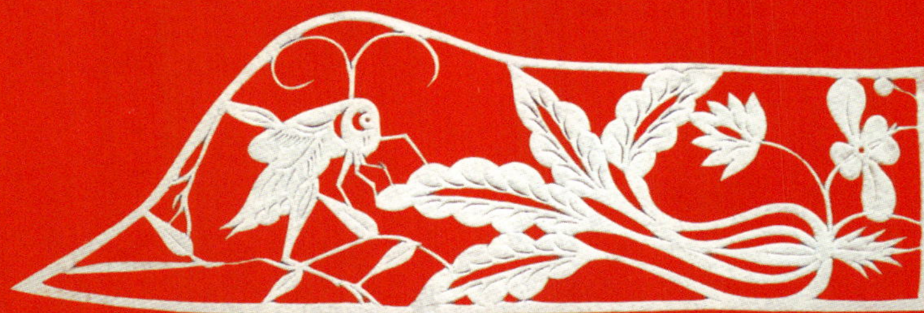

Katydid and Cabbage

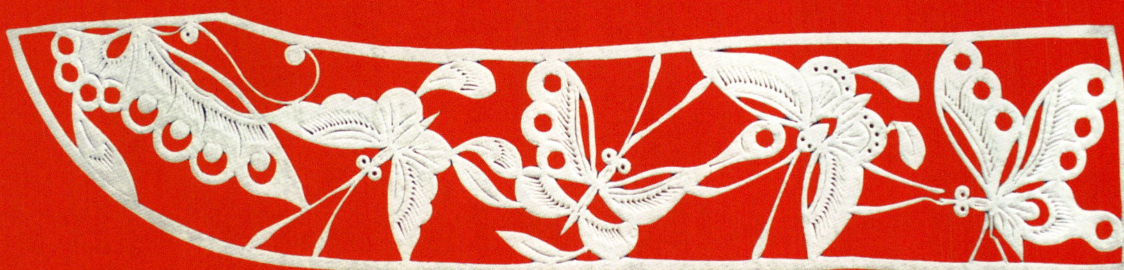

The Butterflies' Dance

These three pictures are all designs for embroidering shoes. These are all designs of popular vegetables and insects. However, they bear another kind of meaning after the arrangement of crafters. The squirrel symbolizes a male and both the grapes and the cabbage symbolize a female. The two butterflies flying wing to wing symbolize two lovers. All together these three designs have the meaning that lovers play together.

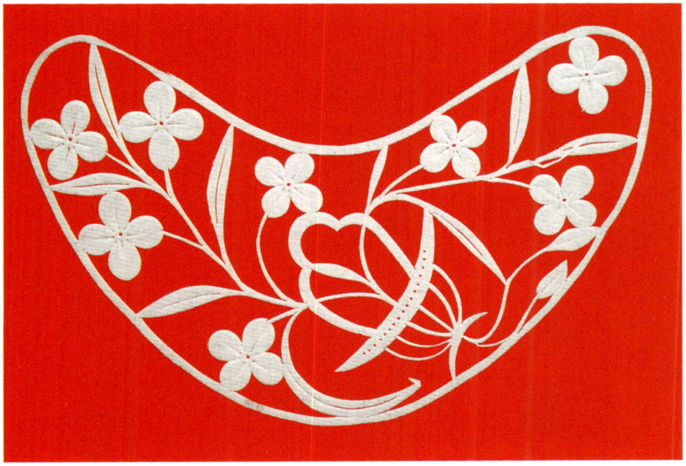

The Sweet-scented Osmanthus

These two are paper-cut designs for the toe of the shoe. This one represents the sweet-scented osmanthus and the other one the cold-resistant chrysanthemum.

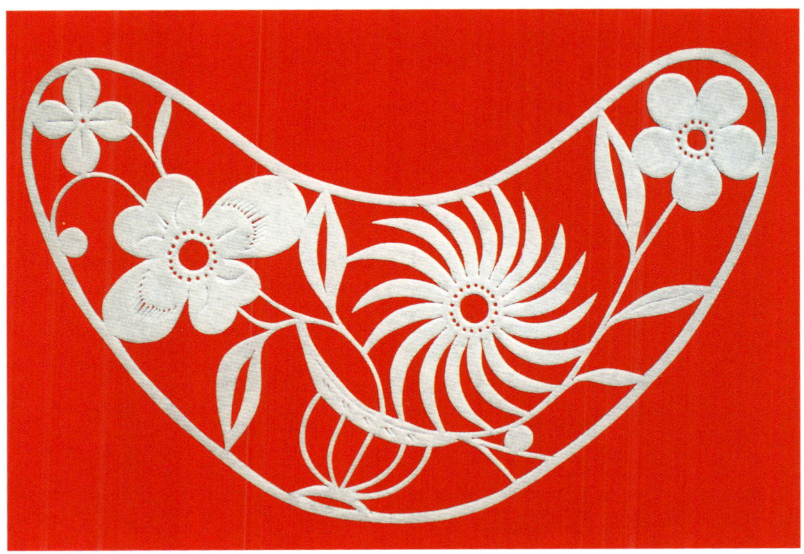

The Chrysanthemum

(ibid)

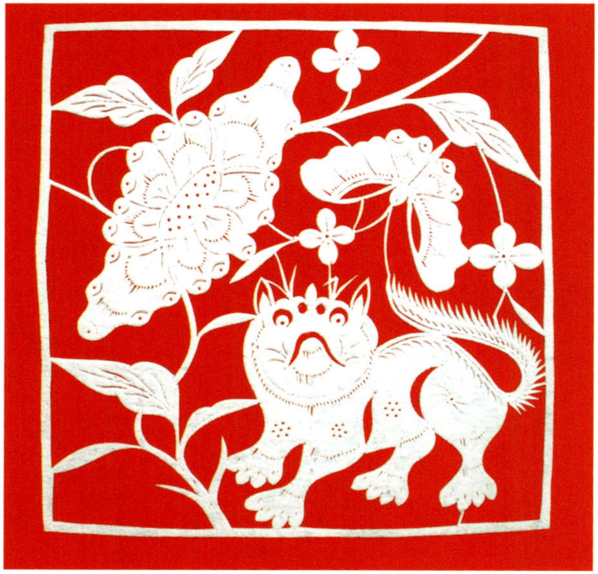

Cat, Butterfly and Peony

This is a design for embroidering pillow covers. In ancient times the age from seventy to eighty is called the Maodie age. In Chinese the cat and the butterfly have the same pronunciation as Maodie, so they represent old age. The peony symbolizes wealth. The combination means that old aged people are rich.

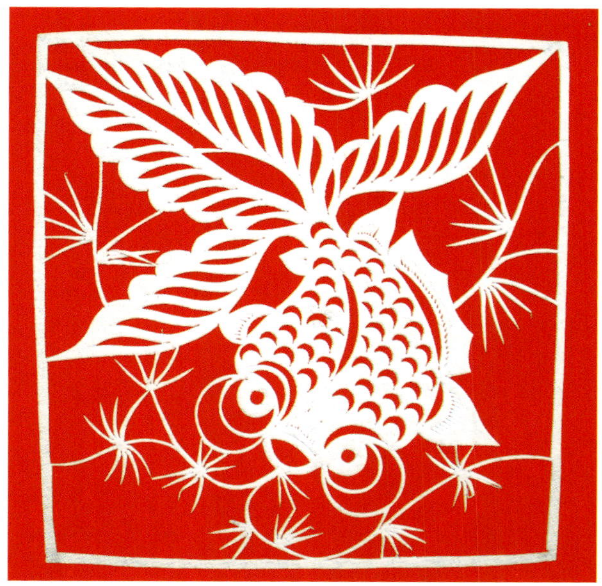

The Goldfish

The Goldfish, design for embroidered pillow covers, symbolizes a hall packed with riches.

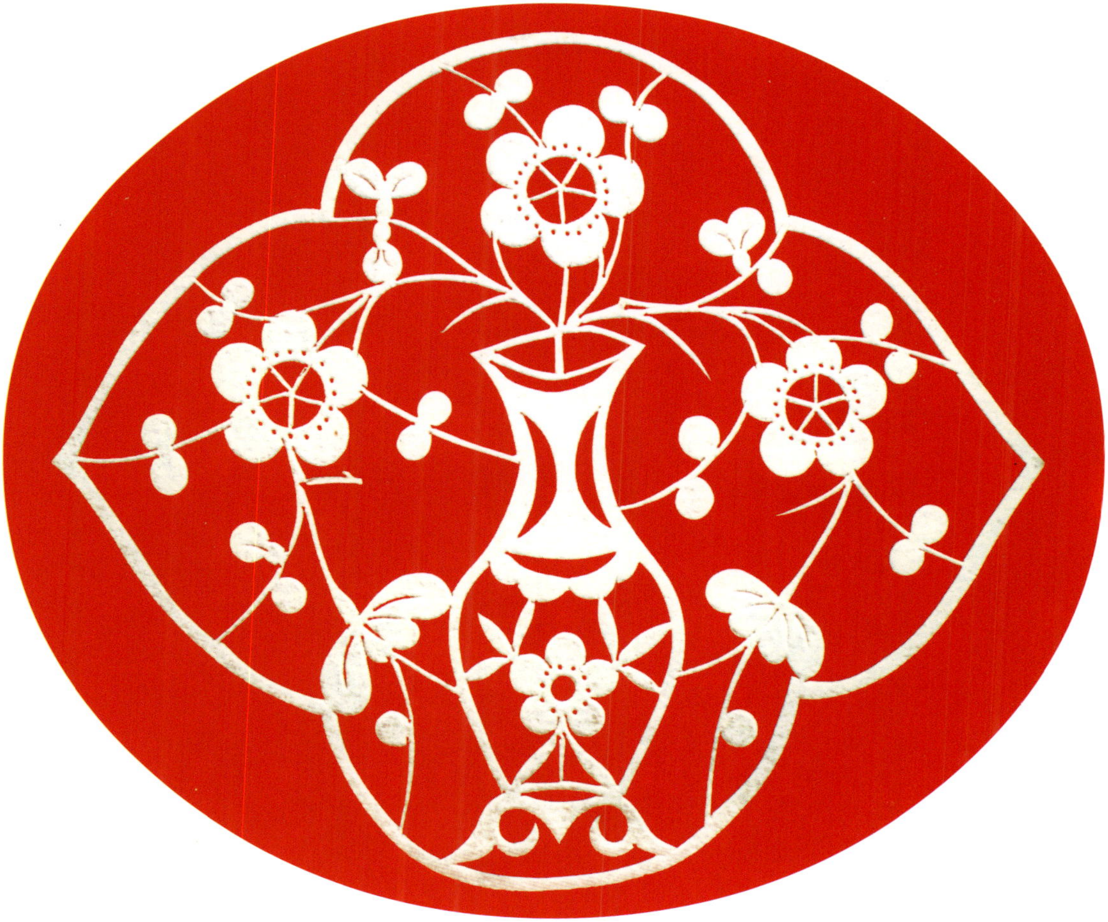

Plum

This is a paper-cut design for embroidering a Hebao bag. Originally the Hebao bag had a similar significance as with gourd dippers. In ancient times there was a wedding ritual. A gourd is normally divided into two dippers and the bride and groom hold one each for drinking water. A girl sends an embroidered Hebao bag to her lover as a pledge of love. It not only carries the meaning that "the fragrance of plum blossom sharpens in the bitter cold," but also urges the lover to ask a matchmaker to propose marriage.

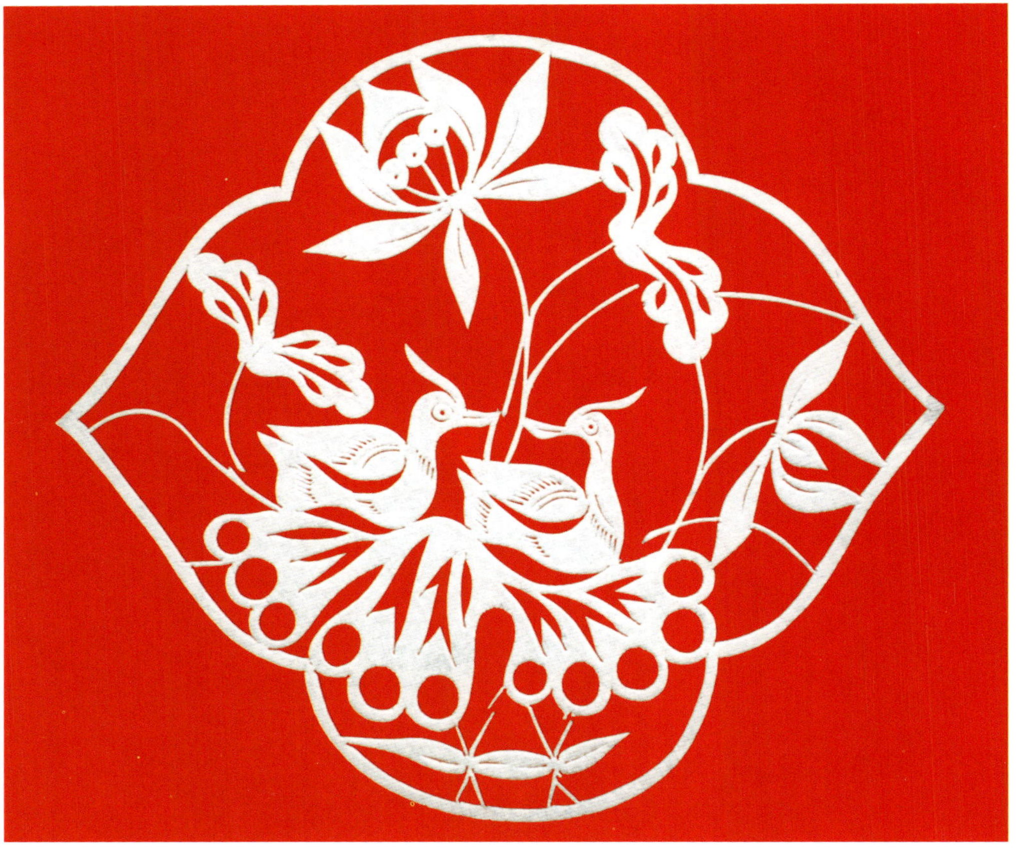

Mandarin Ducks Lying on Lotus Flowers

This is also a paper-cut design for embroidered a Hebao bag. A pair of mandarin ducks never separate, which is a good example for devoted couples. Lotus flowers are also interpreted as giving birth. So the meaning of a girl embroidering a bag with this design is clear.

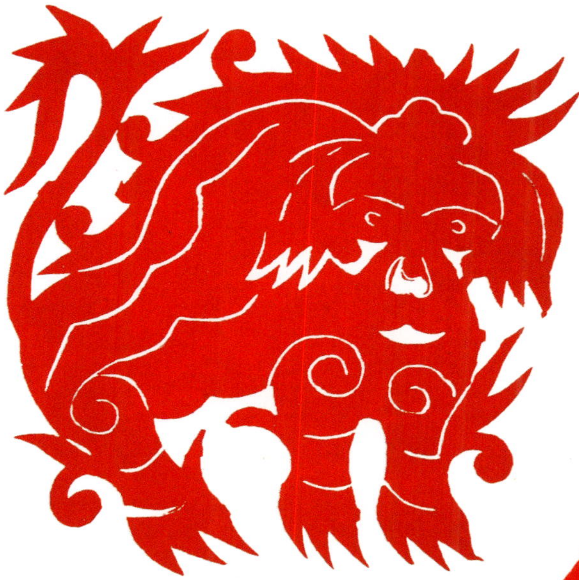

The Lion

This is a design for embroidering the cuff of a jacket within the Miao ethnic group. The lion represents power and auspiciousness.

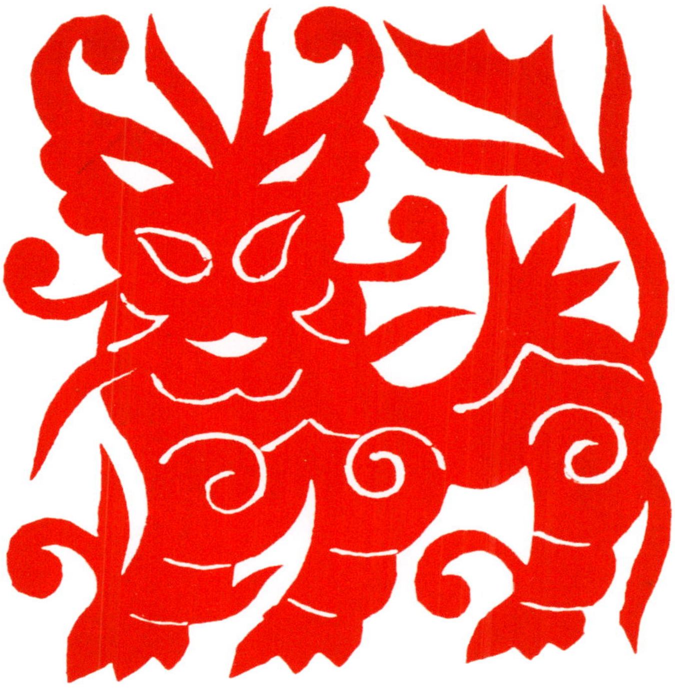

A Tiger with a Dragon's Head

It is a design for embroidering the cuffs of a jacket. The dragon and the tiger are auspicious animals loved by the Chinese people. The former is the master in water and the latter the king on the mountains. Hence the combination is very powerful.

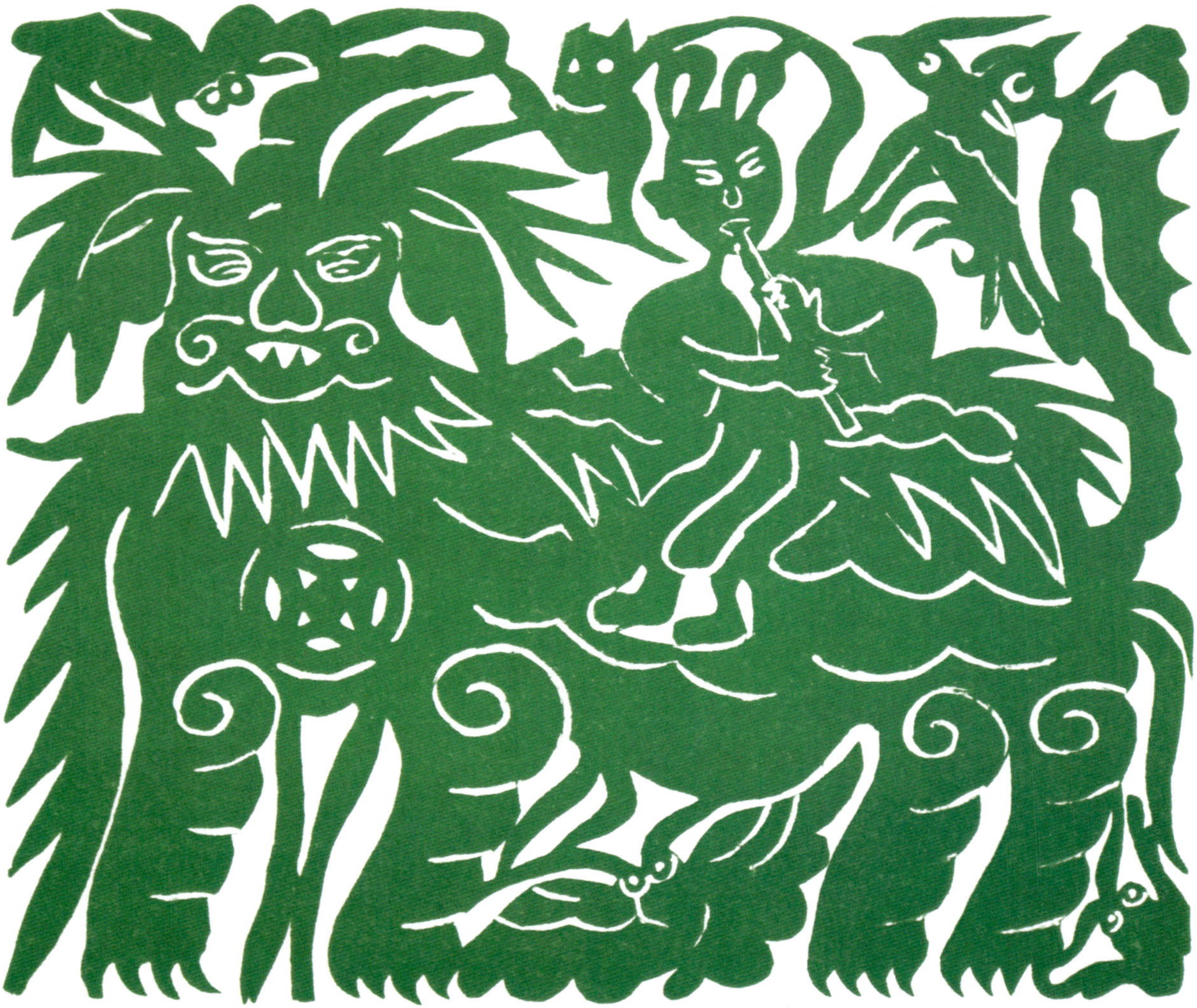

The Lion and the Cowboy

This is also a design for embroidering the cuffs. Even though the lion is fierce he can become friendly with human beings if he is well treated.

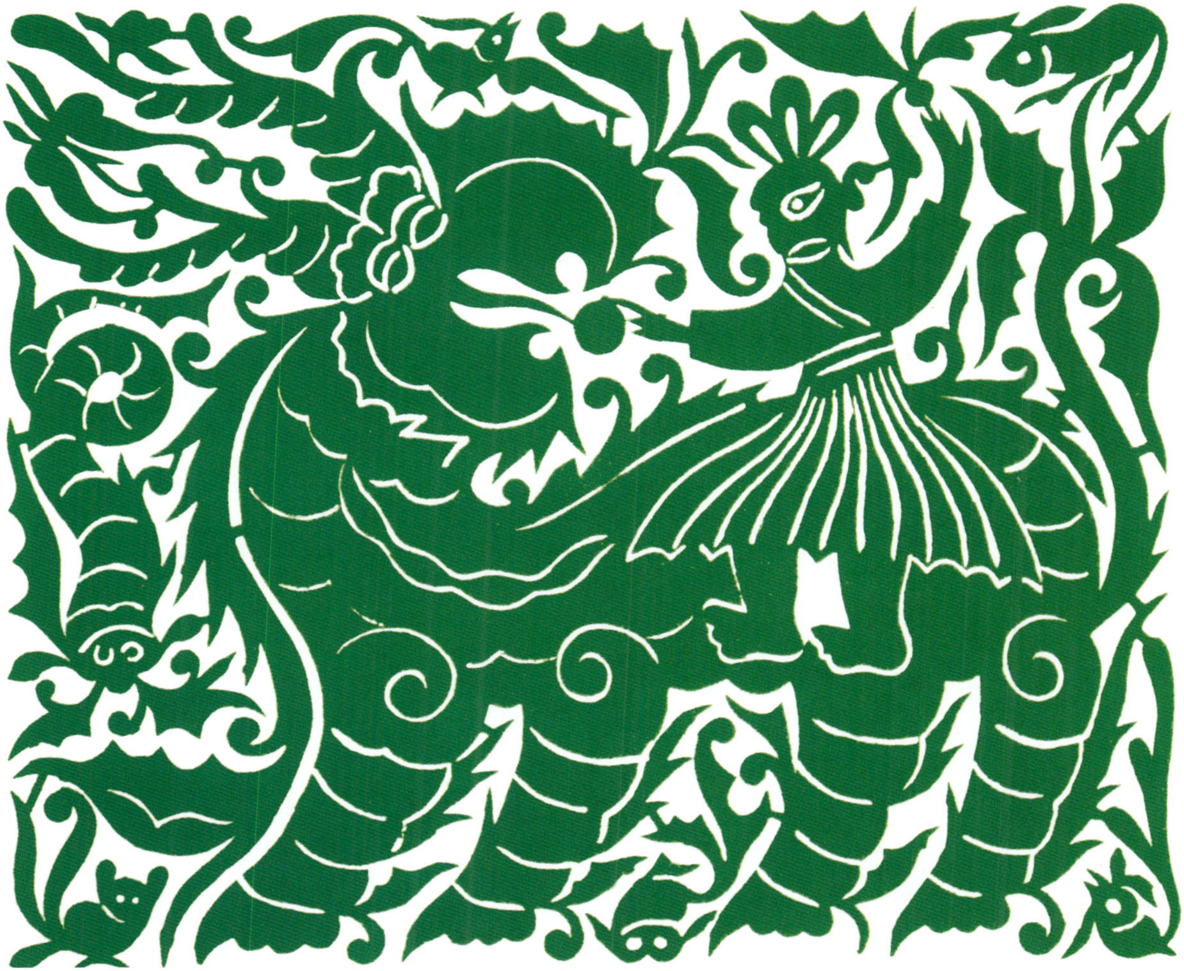

Taming the Dragon Ox

The people of the Miao ethnic group regard the dragon as a divine animal who brings people blessings and luck and the mighty ox as a good co-worker for farming. The combination of the dragon and the ox will prevent the harvest from being ruined by disasters. In addition it is tamed by a female which indicates that females played the leading role in livestock taming in ancient times.This is also a design for embroidering the cuffs.

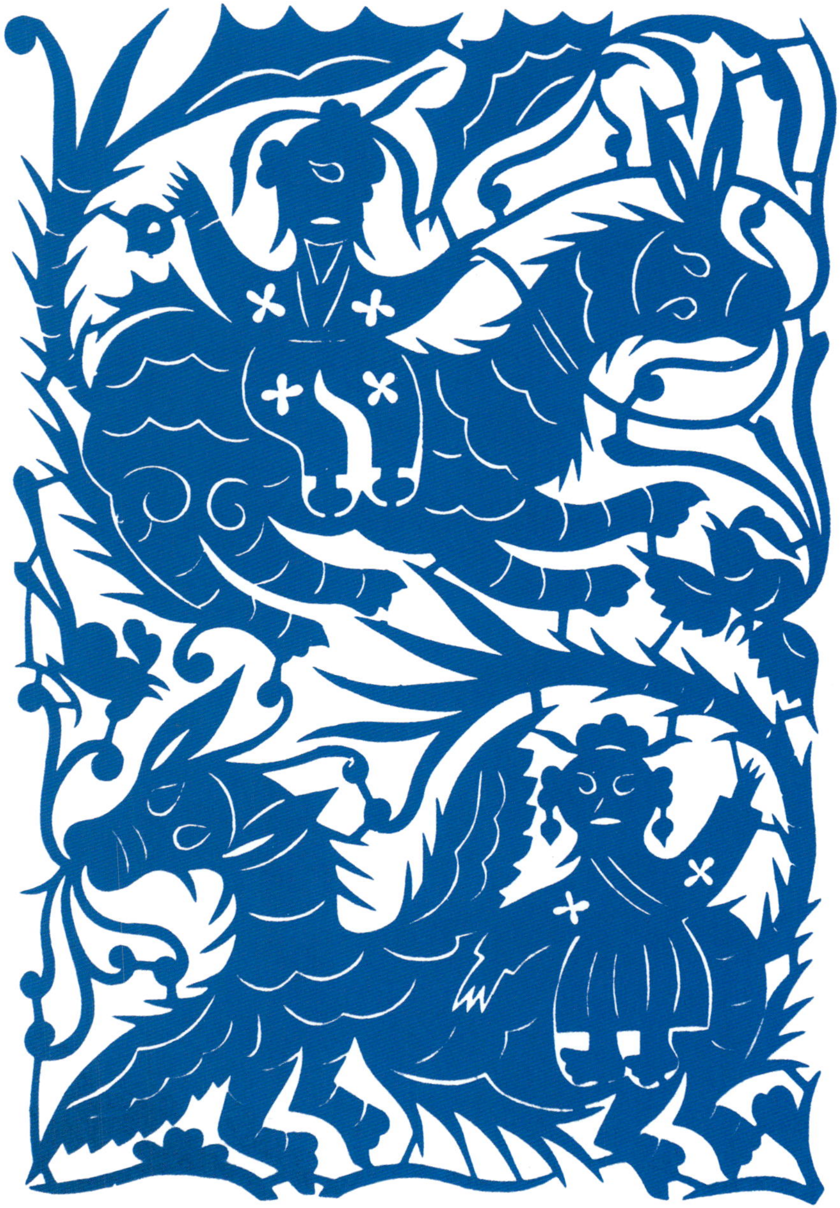

Jiangyang and His Younger Sister Competing in a Horse Race

This is a paper-cut design for embroidering on an apron depicting the fable of the origins of the Miao ethnic group in the distant past.

A long, long time ago there was a great flood which reached up to the sky. All the human beings died except for Jiangyang and his younger sister who hid in a gourd. In order to multiply, they had to get married by a special horse race. The younger sister rode on a Pegasus so Jiangyang could not catch up with her. Clever Jiangyang turned his horse back and met his sister coming the other way and in the end they got married. The picture is extremely ingenious especially the way the two horsetails are detailed. They make the whole picture in an S-shaped design which means the two tails are opposing each other but at the same time complementing each other. It really makes you think when you see it.

Category of Decoration

Embroidery itself is a kind of decoration but why make a "picture of embroidery" and does this belong to such a category? As mentioned before, after the embroidery is completed the paper-cut can not be seen, so how do we decorate? What we are talking about here are the papercuts which are directly used to decorate the environment and utensils. This includes the papercuts used to decorate windows, ceilings, beds and utensils.

The ones used for window decoration are often seen and are normally the richest in terms of content and variety of form. They include lovely precious animals, popular characters in dramas, age old legends and interesting things in life.

These papercuts have a long life normally one year is the shortest length of time. The papercuts used for window decoration are only replaced on the eve of the Chinese New Year. Due to its highly visible position, it demands a high level of craft. They should be both vivid and true. There is a saying amongst the people "there should be a good story in the papercuts used for window decoration so that they are still attractive even though they are seen numerous times."

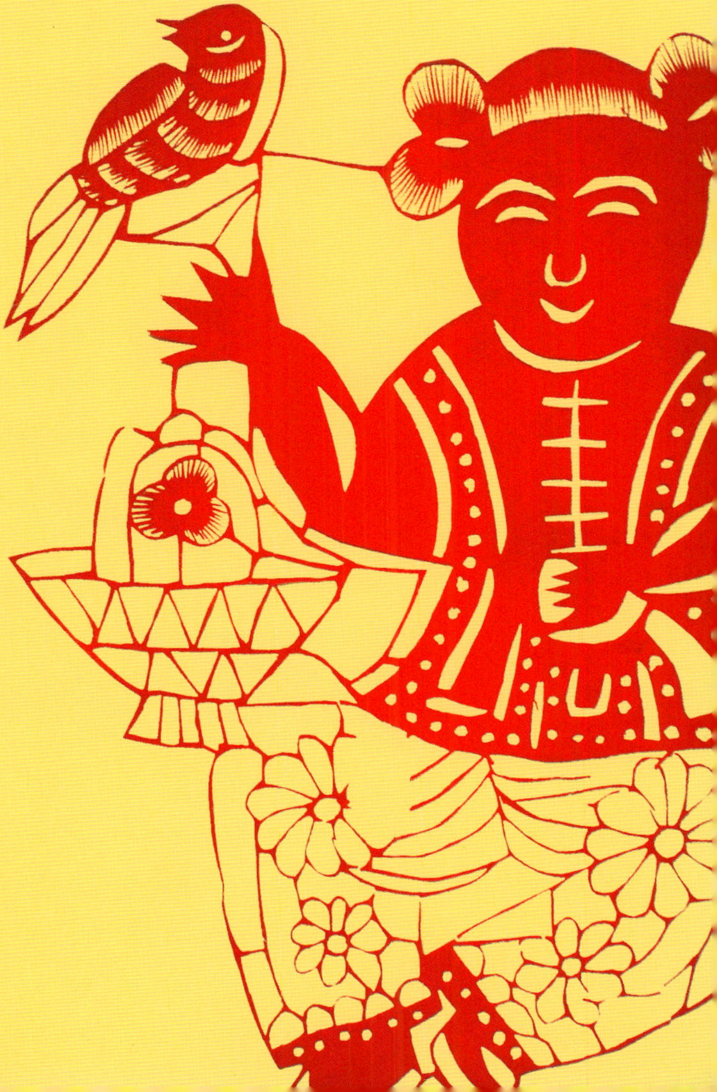

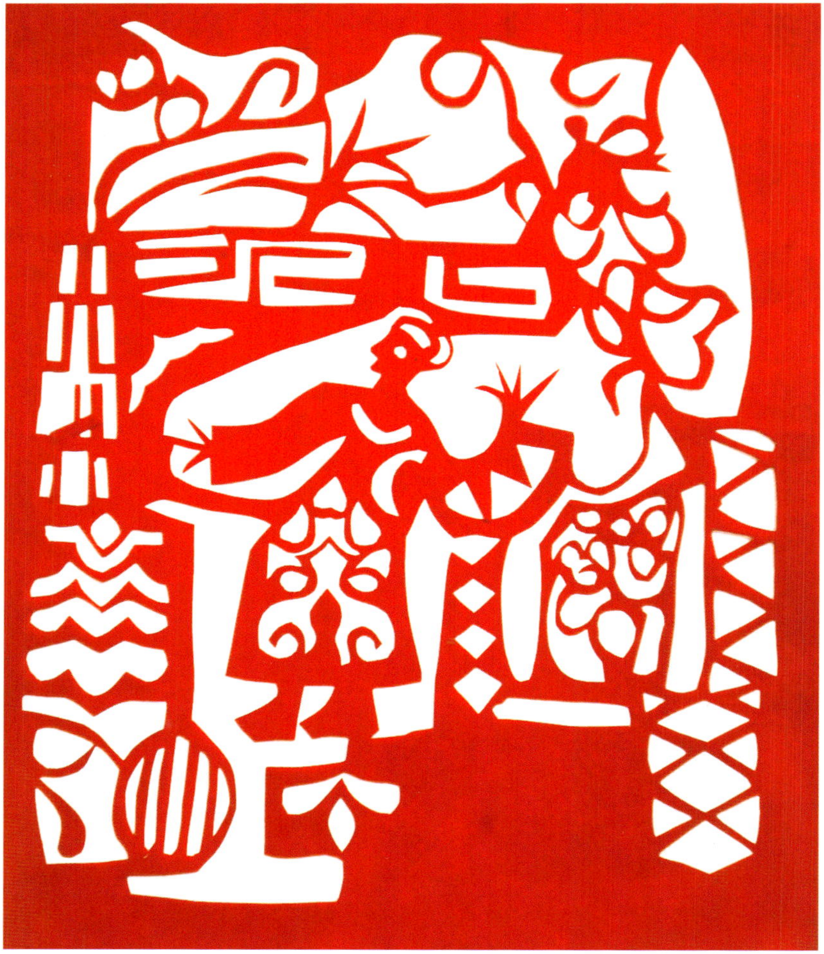

Bridal Chamber

Commonly window flowers are pasted on the window. However, this and the following one are directly pasted onto the lattices of the window and, at the same time, used as vent holes to ventilate the house. A new house is usually built for the wedding of the adult son. After the marriage the bride becomes the housewife of the new house, being in charge of all the housework. The young wife in the picture is busy rearranging her own room.

Greeting

When her husband returns after work she greets him and helps him to get rid of the dust and to change his clothes. How warm the small family is!

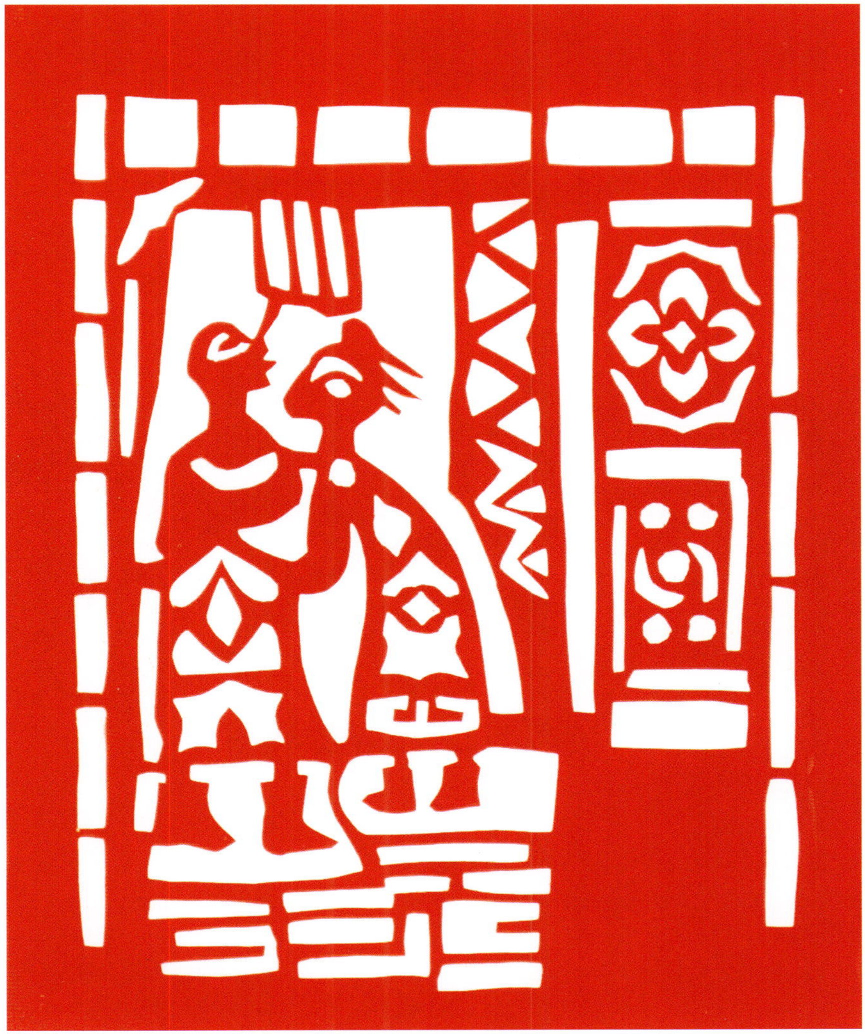

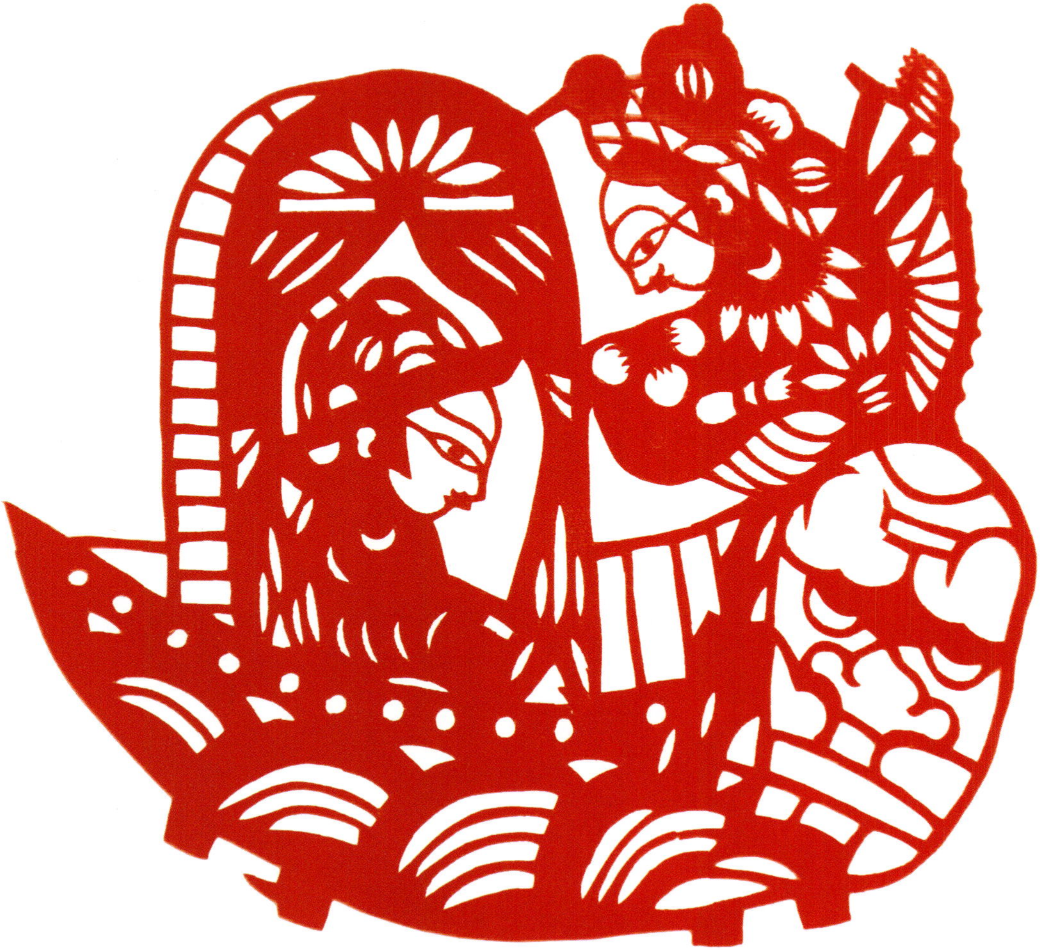

Going Into Hiding

The folk arts are chiefly inherited and created by women. Not only should they be well acquainted with various fables, legends and historical stories, but also should express them with artistic styles in different forms. In fact the house is an exhibition hall and a platform. The paper cuts for windows and bed decoration are works and teaching materials created and compiled by them (the women).

Huadan

Huadan is one of the main female characters in Beijing opera.

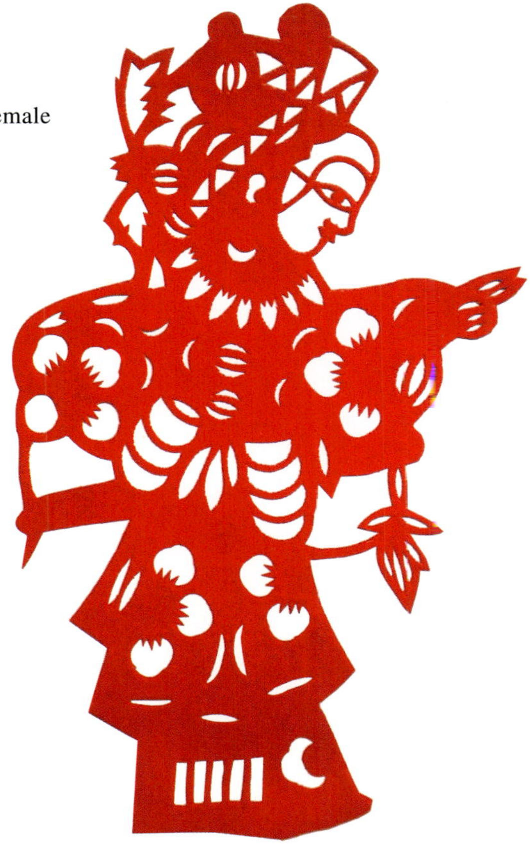

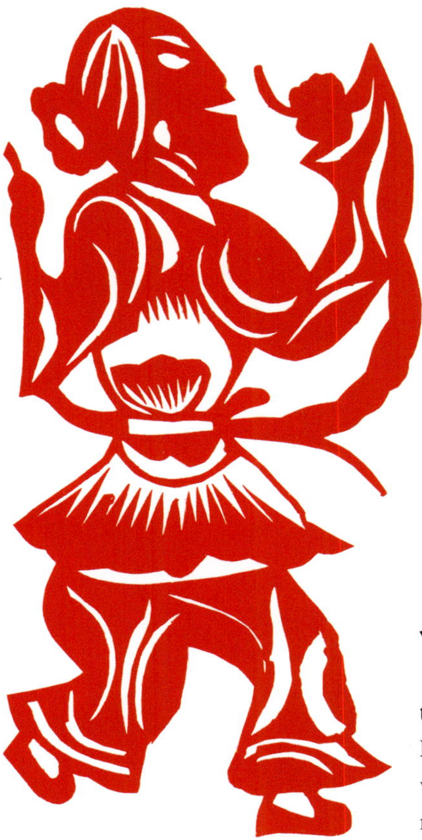

Yangge (popular rural folk dance)

It is difficult for modern people living in urban areas to imagine the expectation and the special feeling of the people towards the New Year in the past. Especially the joy in their participation in Yangge and other art performances would last for several days. Hence, they cut a paper and pasted it with a view to retaining the cheerful atmosphere of the dance.

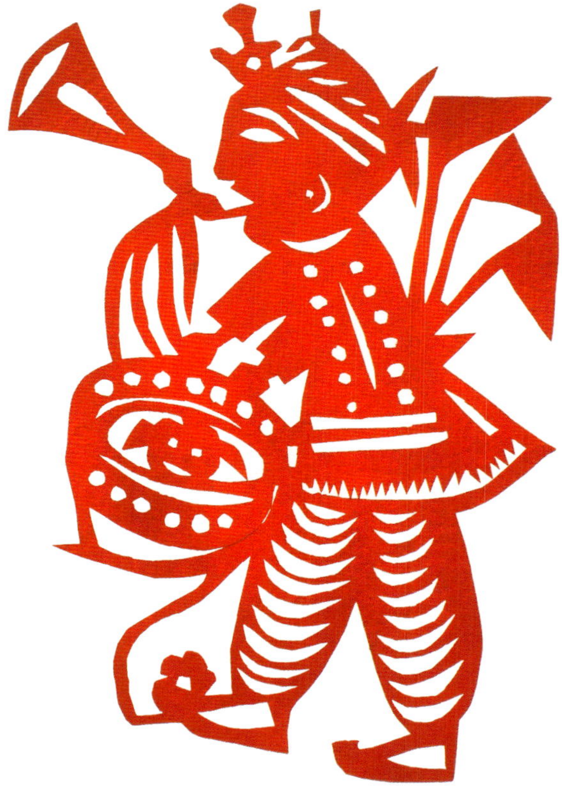

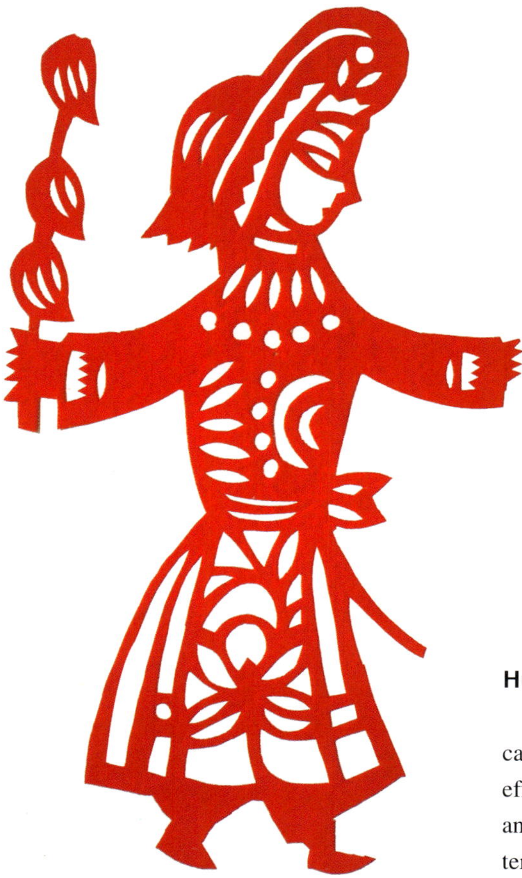

Hua Mulan

This is a paper cut-out of Hua Mulan, a character in opera. If studied carefully she seems to be walking with quick short steps. Such a visual effect is caused by the five swinging vertical lines of skirts and the up and down tiptoes. How carefully the author of this work observes characters and how accurately he/she gets the expression.

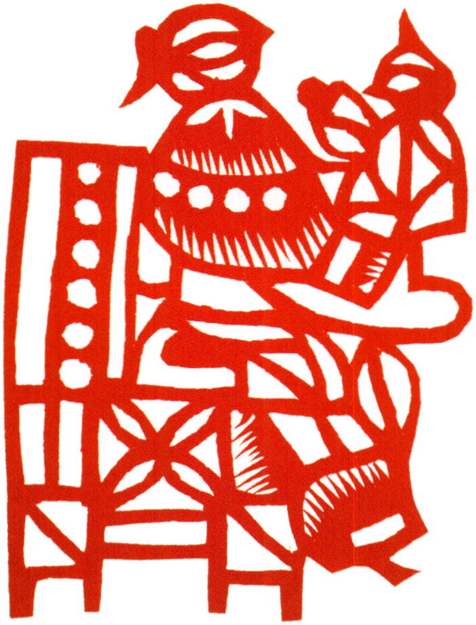

Playing with a Grandson

It is a great pleasure for elders to play with grandchildren. In the picture the little grandson, with no sense of malice, tries to scratch the face of the grandma who quickly avoids his fingers.

Weaving

This has been a part of life for several thousand years as well as a synonym for the farming culture. Frequent weavings indicate ample food and clothing. In the picture the girl weaves to the sound of rhythmic songs. Moreover, the crafty four sides bring you to the front of the "window of a farmhouse."

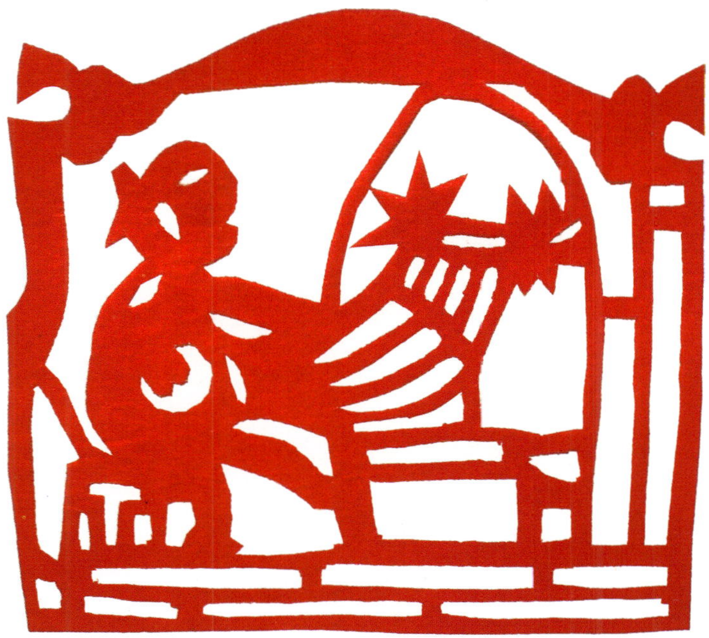

Roles of Beijing Opera include the five—Sheng, Dan, Jing, Mo and Chou. The face of Jing is painted most colorfully. This is why Beijing opera masks produced in Weixian County of Hebei Province are mostly Jing ones.

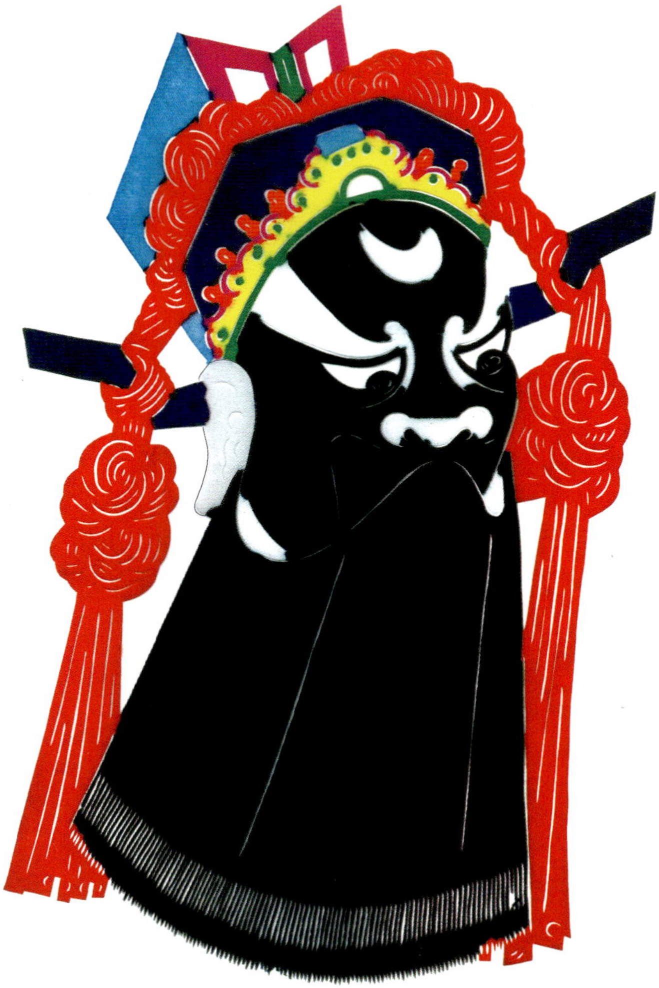

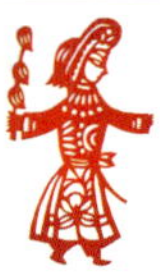

Lord Bao

Impartial and incorruptible, Lord Bao is not scared of influential officials. He is upright and outspoken; he is always on the side of the people. He is a just and upright official as well as a "star" in the minds of the people. His virtue is widespread among the people. Hence, cutting a paper in the shape of Lord Bao would not only adore him as the modern idolaters paste the pictures of "pop stars," but also enable stories and legends regarding him to be told to the children.

Dou Erdun

Dou Erdun is a forest hero, chivalrous and having a strong hatred of evil practices. He is highly praised and taken as a main character in various dramas. Designs on these two paper-cuttings draw experiences from facial make-ups in opera.

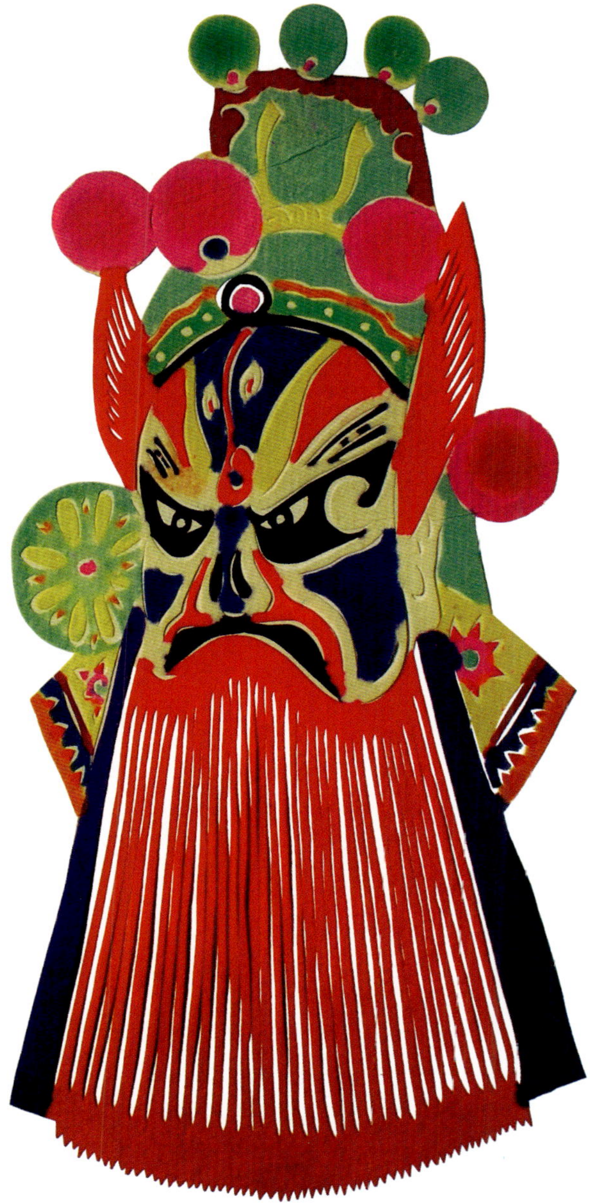

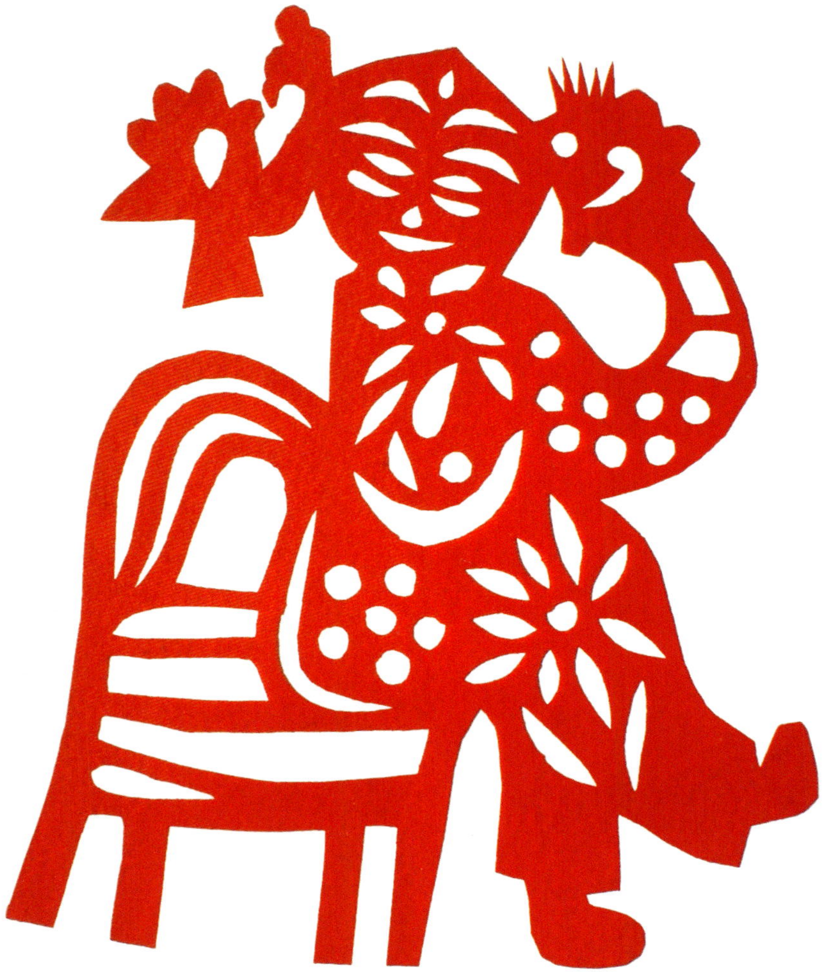

A Girl Wearing Flowers on Her Head

It is the nature of young girls to be fond of dressing and making up. In the picture is a young girl wearing flowers on her head. The vivid posture in sitting completely reveals her joyful mood: sticking out her chest, turning her head on one side and sitting cross-legged and moving the tips of her toes up and down. It shows us a clever and eccentric girl.

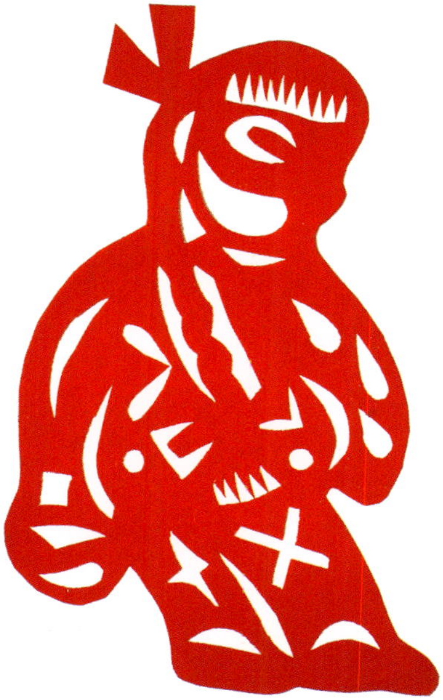

A Girl Wearing Her Hair in Plaits

This is a young girl who is combing out her hair. She is totally different from the above girl in character: the former "clever and eccentric" and the latter " honest and kind." How does the "inside" character come out? Does it relate to the object lines? The lines of the former have obvious turns, bright and vivid; those of the latter are straight and curving alternatively, gentle and simple. It is the magical function of lines in Chinese art, not only drawing the outline, but also expressing the vivid image and energy of the matter as well as the feeling and interest of the authors. All of those are formed by the changes of lines, straight and curving, gentle and firm and pausing and transiting alternatively.

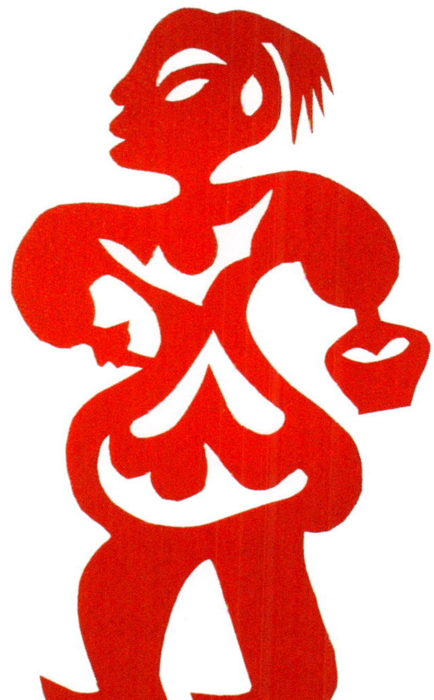

Feeding Hens

How vivid this is! The girl lifts her head and calls the hens in the distance holding a basin in the left hand and sprinkling grains with right hand.

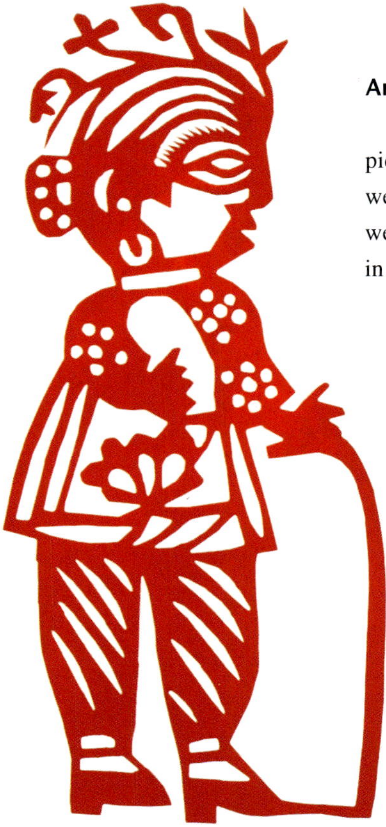

An Old Woman

Though leaning on a stick the old woman in the picture stands straight and looks strong-bodied. She is well dressed with ornaments and bright clothes. Is she welcoming relatives in front of the door or taking part in her grandson's wedding?

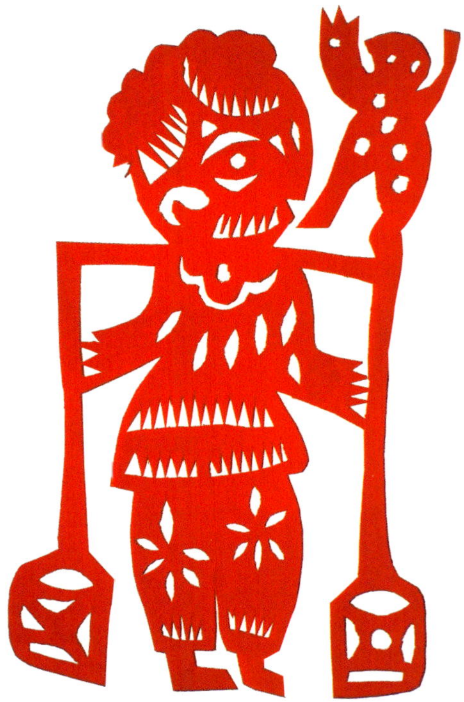

Carrying a Child

This woman is carrying meals out to the workers in the fields on a shoulder pole. However, there is no one to take care of the child so she has to carry the child on the pole. It seems that the little child is scared of nothing, playing cheerfully on the pole.

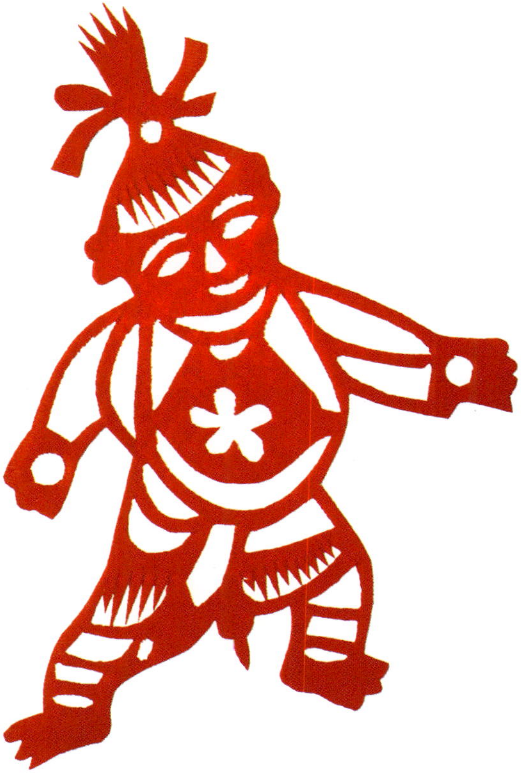

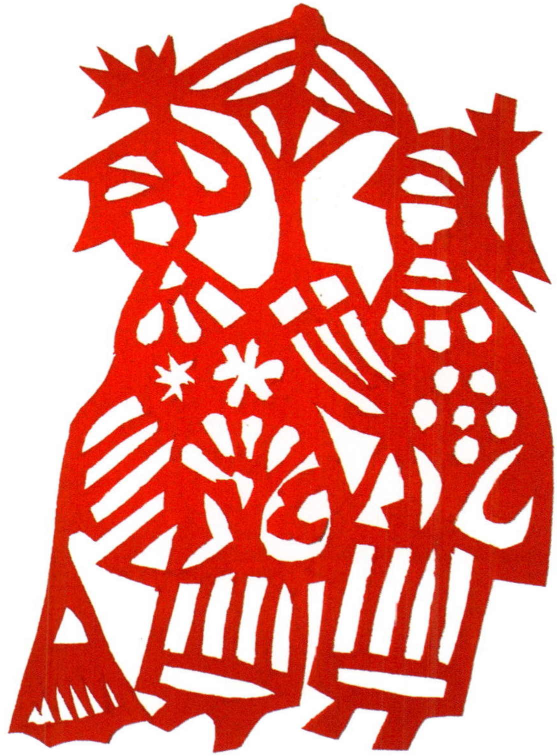

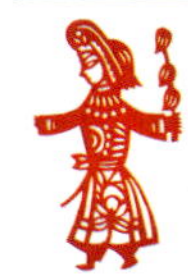

"Stone"

The wide lines of this paper-cut are moderate in both rigidity and density. The boys from farming families named "stone" or "Tiedan" come into being vividly in it.

Holding an Umbrella

Two girls share the same umbrella.

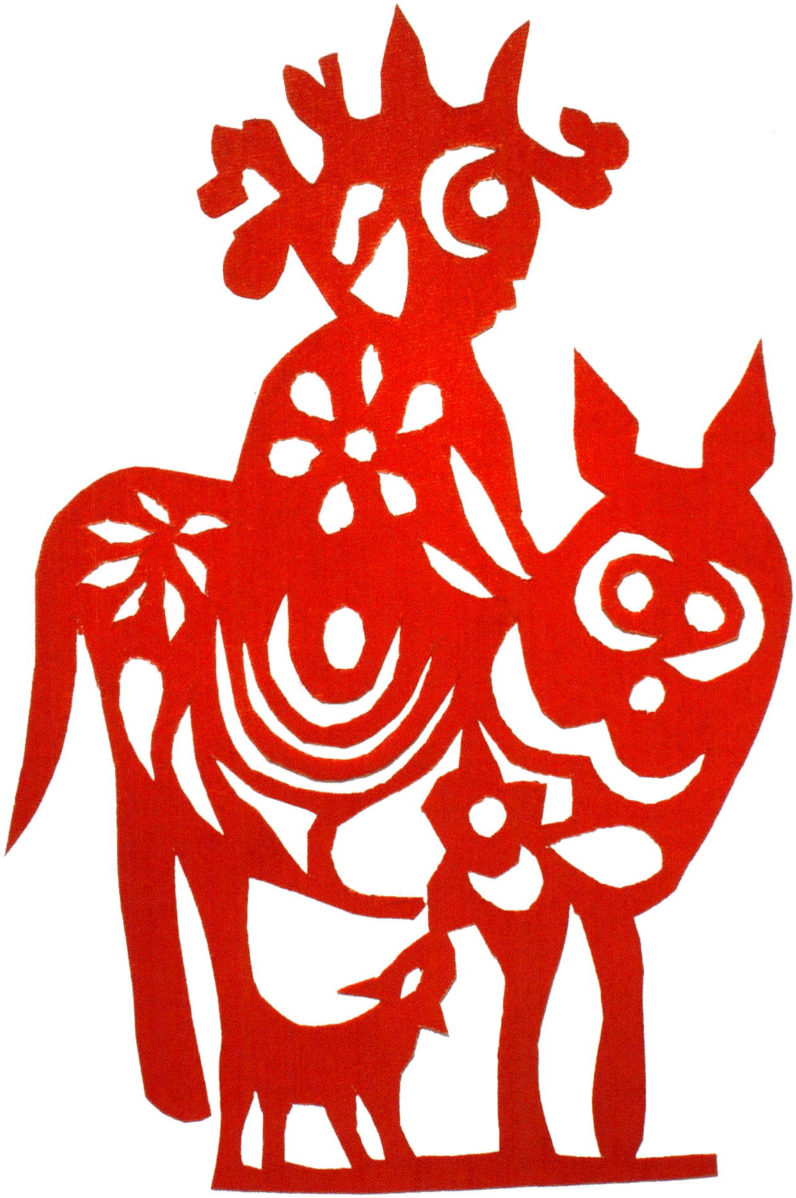

Visiting Relatives

On the loess plateau a woman is seen riding on a donkey to visit relatives. This middle-aged woman is wearing festive clothes with fully decorated headgear. According to tradition she must be going back to her parent's home to take part in her younger brother's wedding.

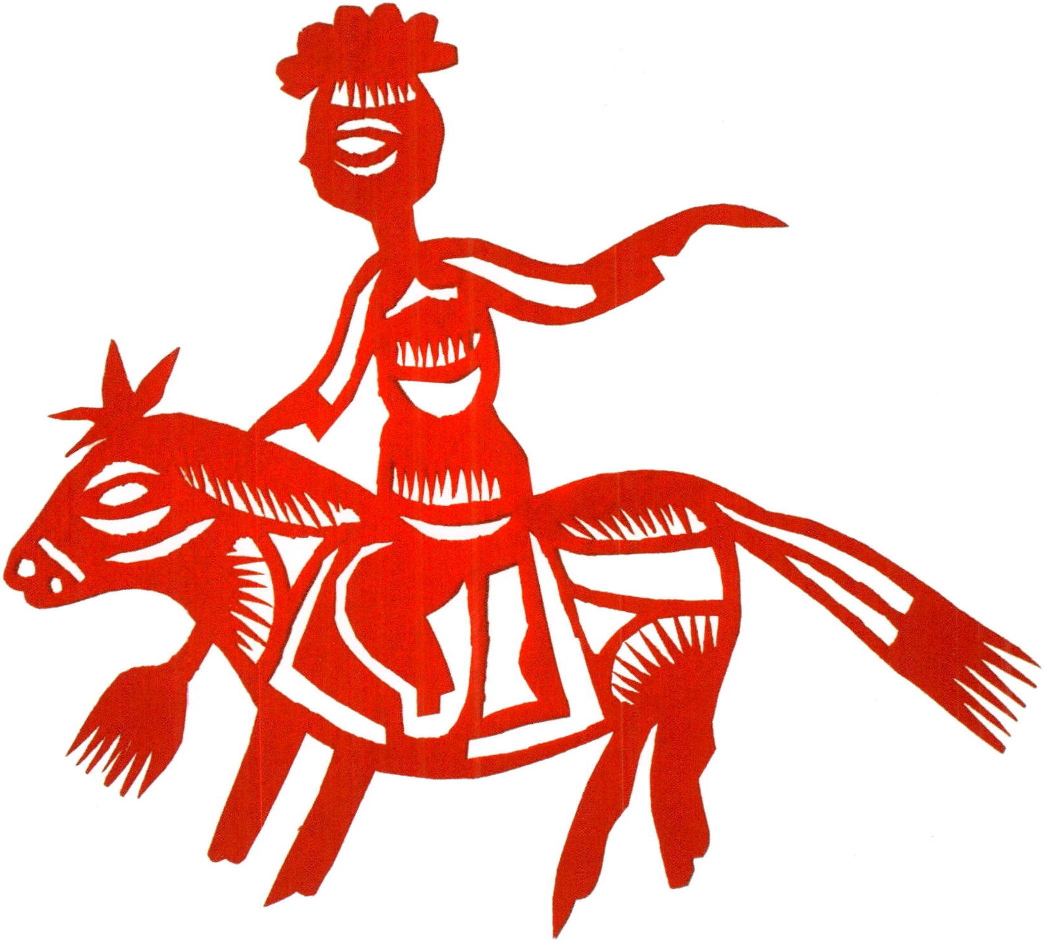

Horse Race

Is the person riding on a swift horse going to visit his relatives or to compete in a horse race? This is not important. What the author really cares about is the gesture and expression of the person when he is speeding on a horse. The gesture is simple because it can be expressed in shape. However, the expression is hard to represent. It cannot be shown or seen either on the body and muscles of the person nor on the horse. Thanks to the graceful lines connecting the arms of the person to the horse, the rhythm and expression in running is to be seen vividly.

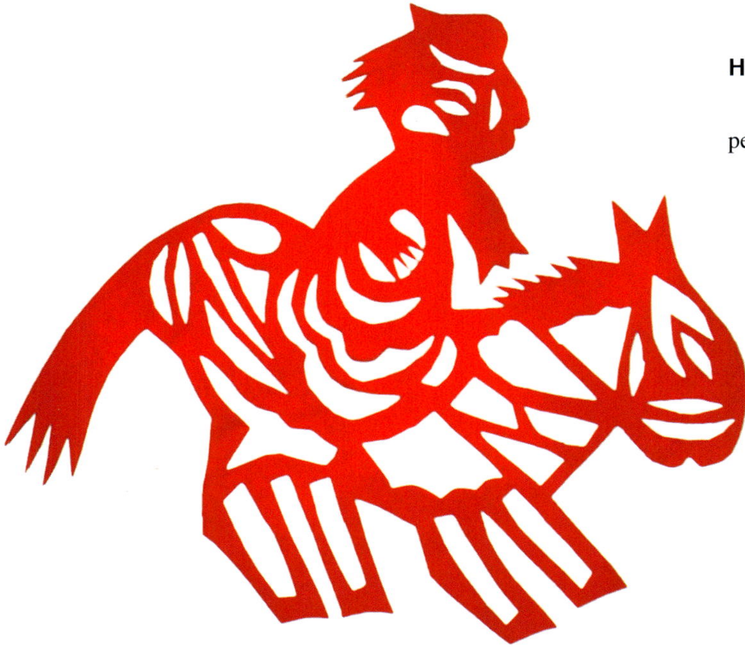

Horse Race

The forelock and backward-flying hair of the person on the horse indicates his speed.

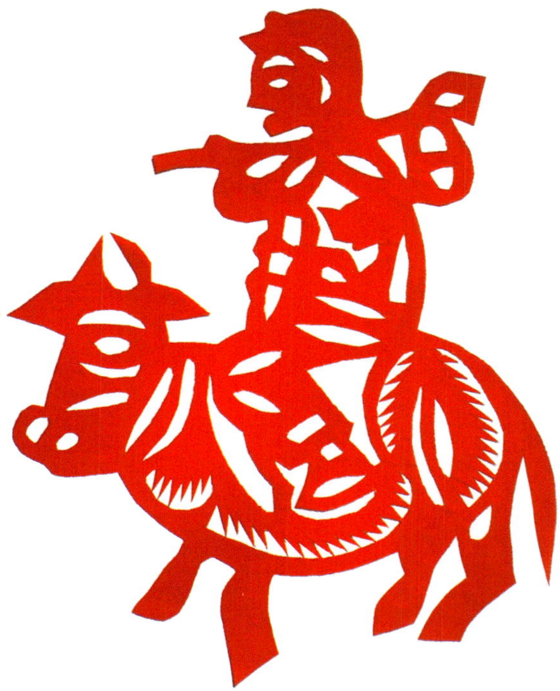

In the Farmland

The ox in the farmland walks slowly and the person is chatting with it. It is certainly not the busy season in farming. This picture shows a leisurely scene in farming life.

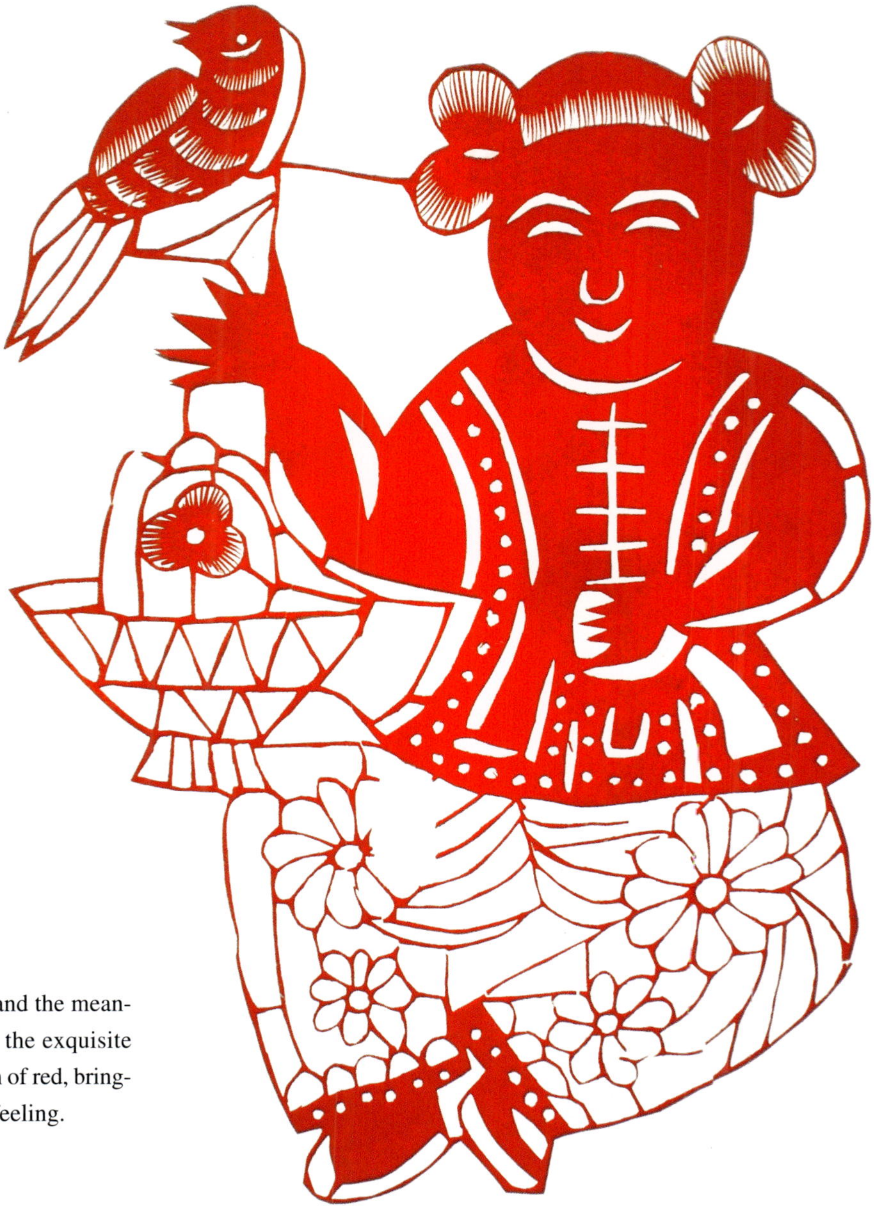

Girl

There is no need to understand the meaning of this work. Just appreciate the exquisite and forceful lines in a large stretch of red, bringing you a clear, bright and pure feeling.

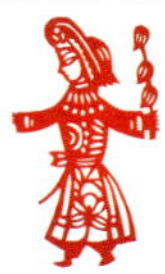

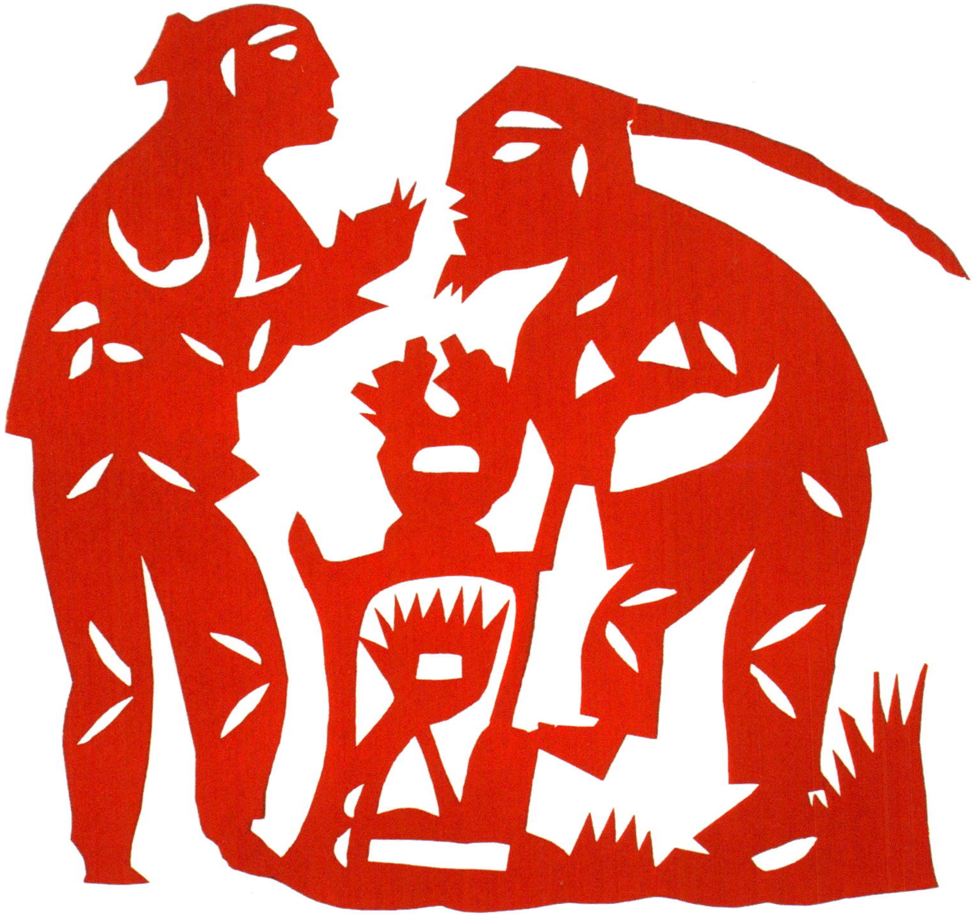

Chattering Endlessly

In the picture is an old couple are talking about something. Indeed older woman are used to chattering endlessly. The old man is tired of listening to his wife chatting but the woman still goes on babbling energetically. From the sticking-up plait of the old man we can see that he is not going to bear it for much longer. All the feelings it brings us are expressed by the accurate object lines.

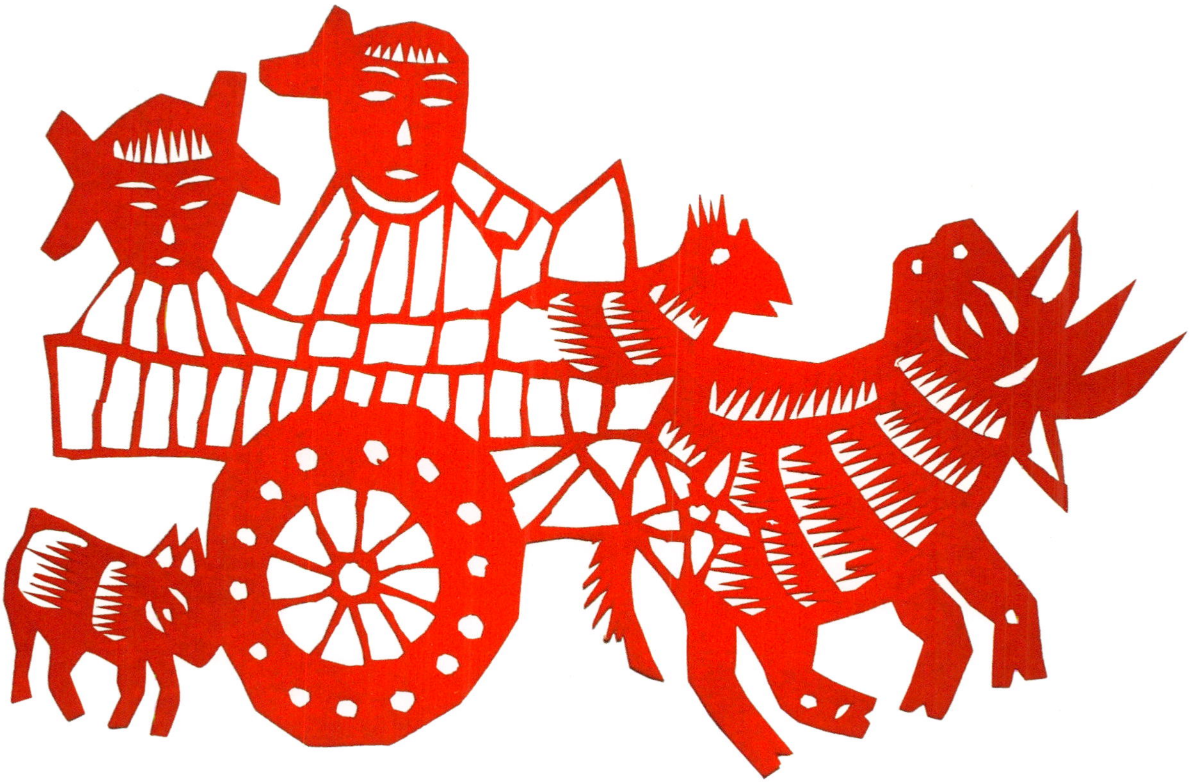

A married woman on the Way to Her Parent's Home

Women take charge of all the housework, including weaving, cooking, sewing and washing. It is a holiday for women to go back to her parent's home. However, there is no one to take over the housework so they must carry the children, sheep, chickens and ducks along with them. Still, even the little ox driving the carriage feels happy.

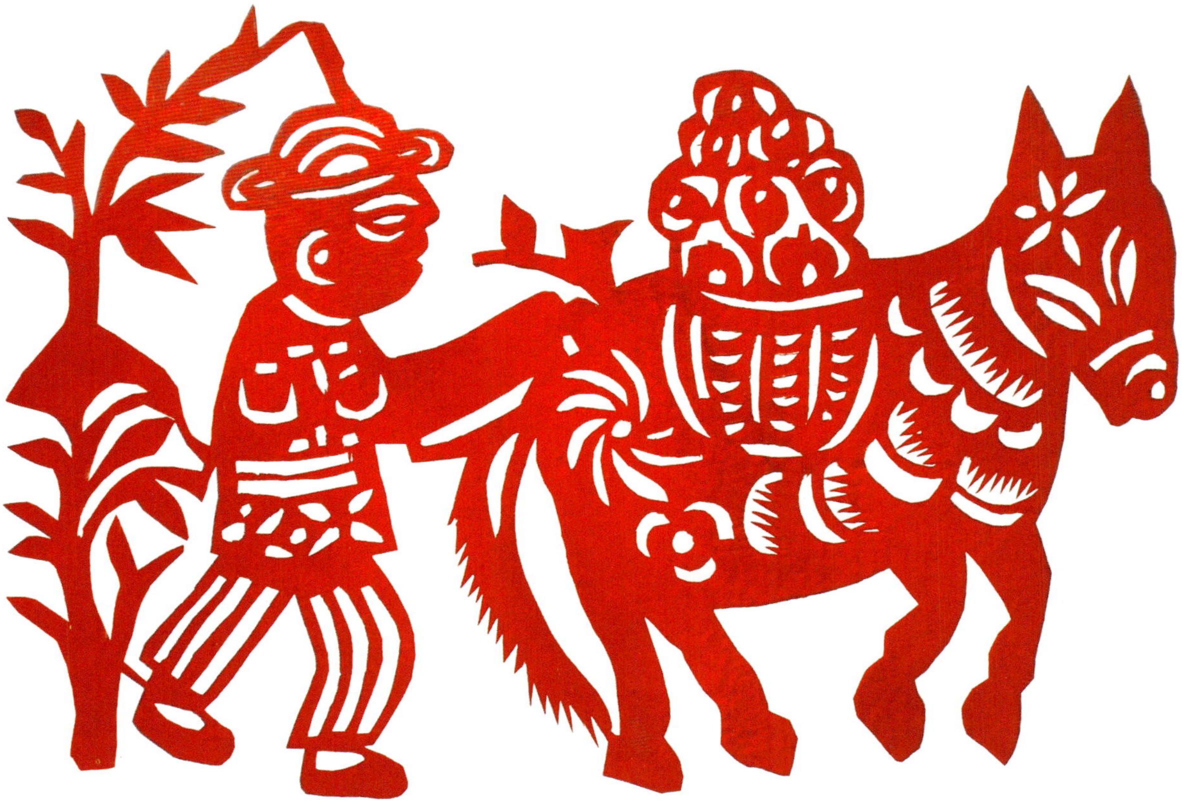

Fruit Harvest

How to describe an apple harvest which has not been finished for dozens of days? The fruit-growing woman has an idea. The person and donkey in the picture are dragging their legs to work.

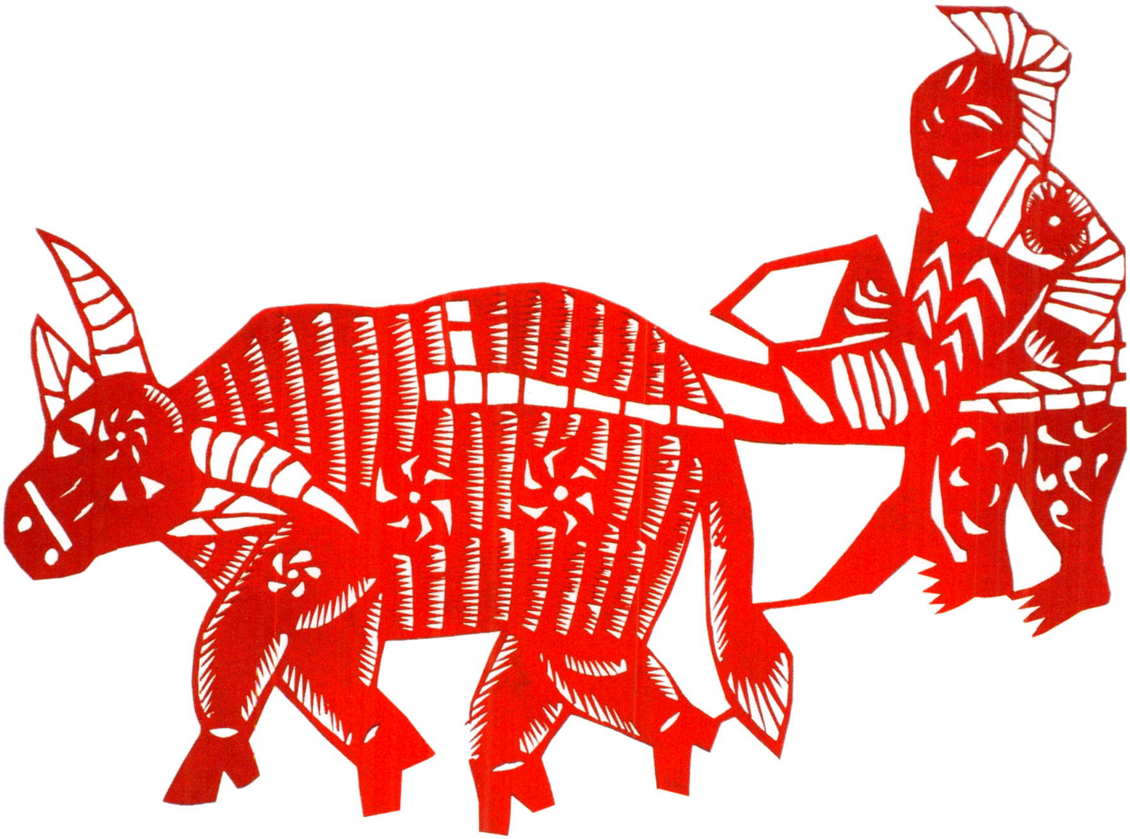

Spring Ploughing

Spring ploughing is the hardest work but it doesn't matter. Though the ox strides neither fast nor slow its forceful steps and large body demonstrate it has enough strength to cope with the work.

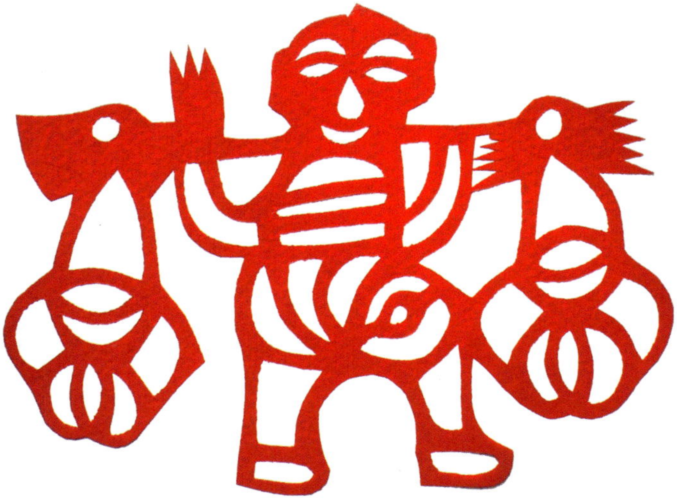

Carrying Meals

The picture depicts a person going to the fields with meals. Because the author uses several camber lines by the two jars in the front and back respectively, it gives us the impression that the person is walking. This is just the magic function of lines in Chinese art.

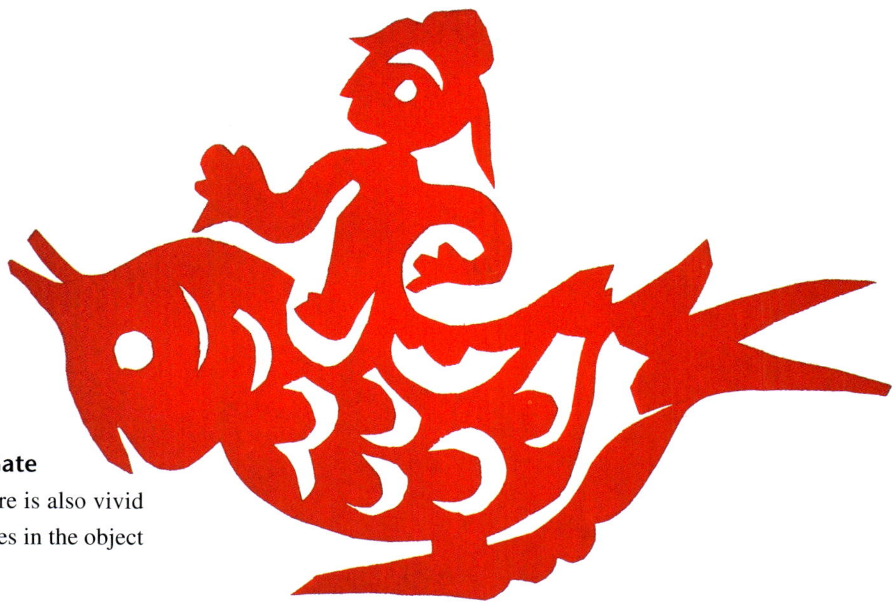

Leaping over the Dragon Gate

The character in this picture is also vivid and this is due to various changes in the object lines.

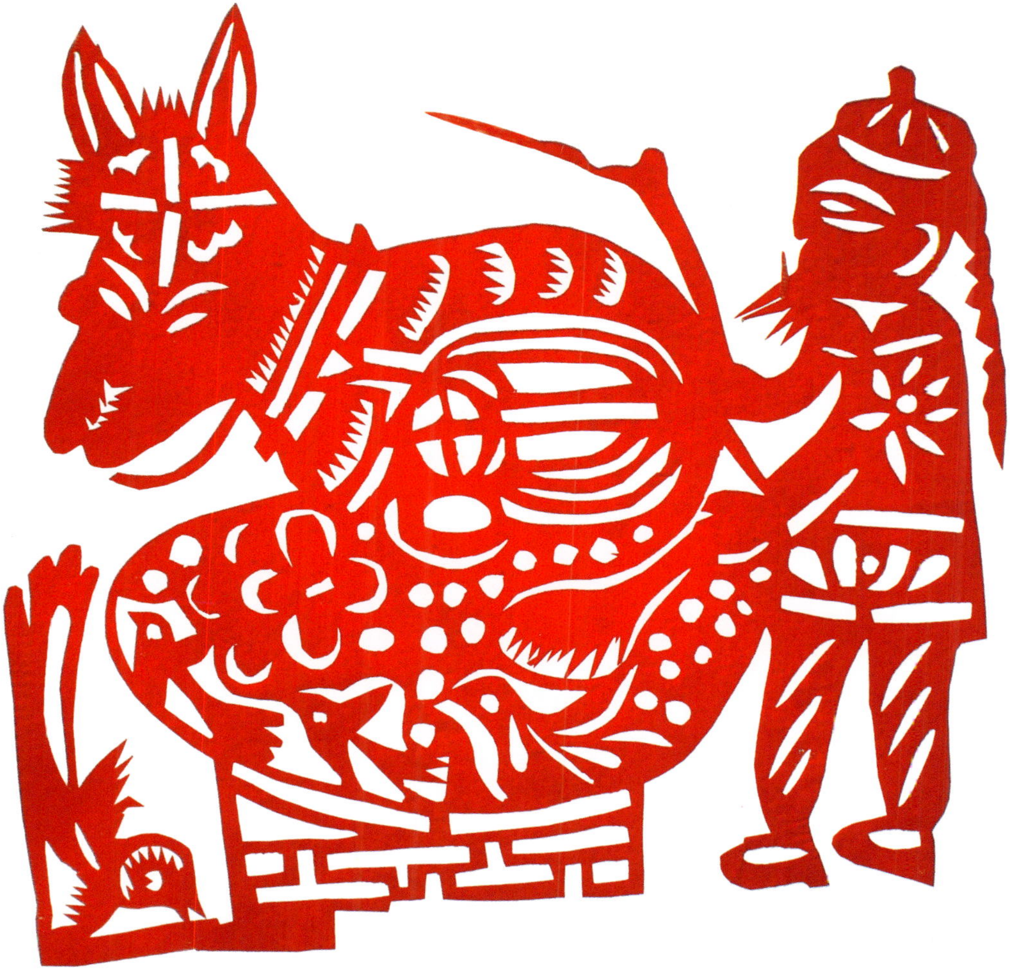

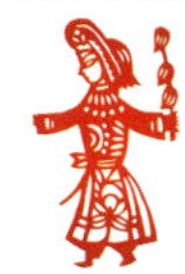

Pulling a Roller

The roller is used to get rid of the grain husks which are then collected and stored in a warehouse. People feel happier if they have to pull the roller for a long time because it indicates a big grain harvest. Even the magpies come to grab the grains. This work not only shows a scene in life, but also expresses the happy mood of the author.

A Mule Carrying Wealth

After seeing this picture, you will be asking, "Does the old woman in the countryside also advocate fauvism?" Of course not, it is the Chinese traditional imagism that "establishes an image to express ideas." A mule completely equipped with saddle and screens symbolizes that the family is rich. In addition, there is a "money bag" which symbolizes an endless source of wealth. Roundness and completion of matters are what the farming families expect. Hence, even the eye of the mule should not be omitted.

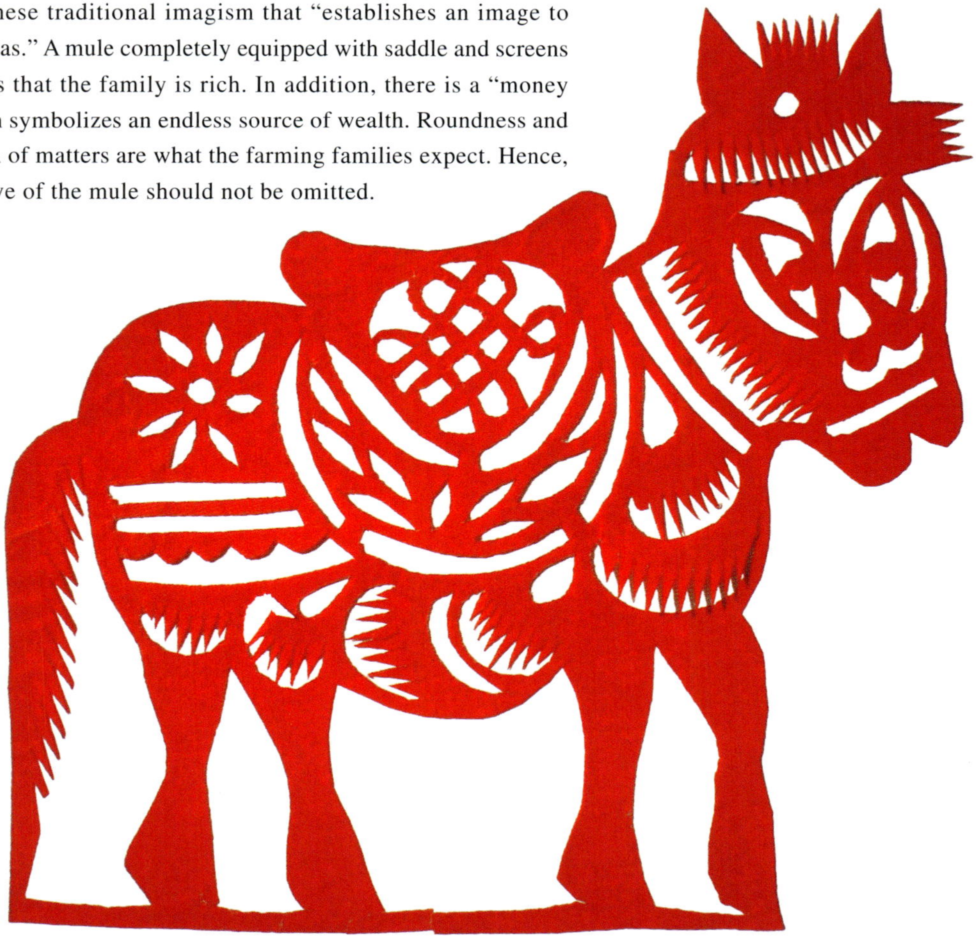

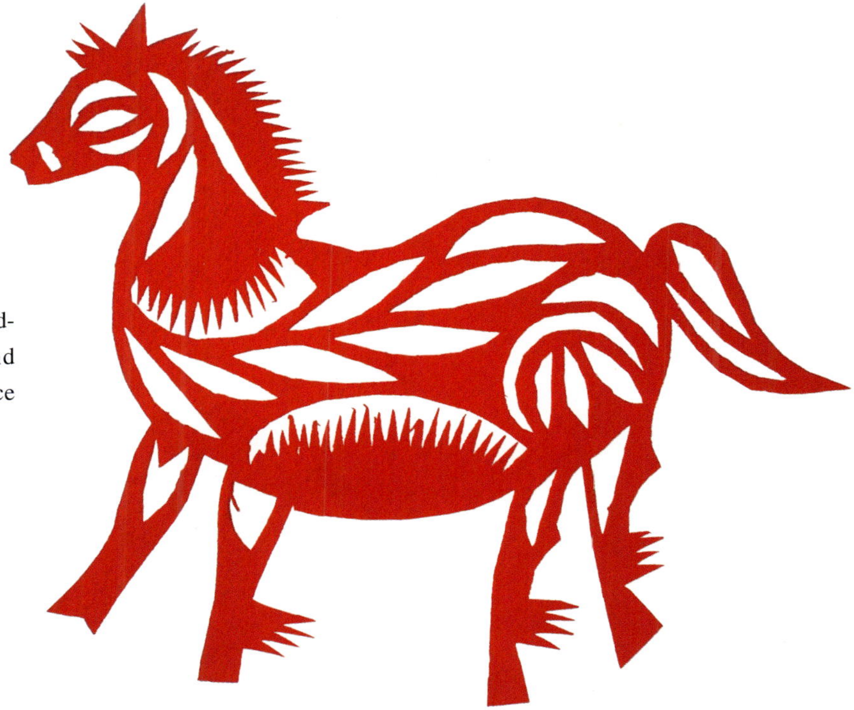

A Fine Horse

In the picture is a fine horse standing against the wind, valiant and vigorous. The impressive appearance finds expression in magic lines.

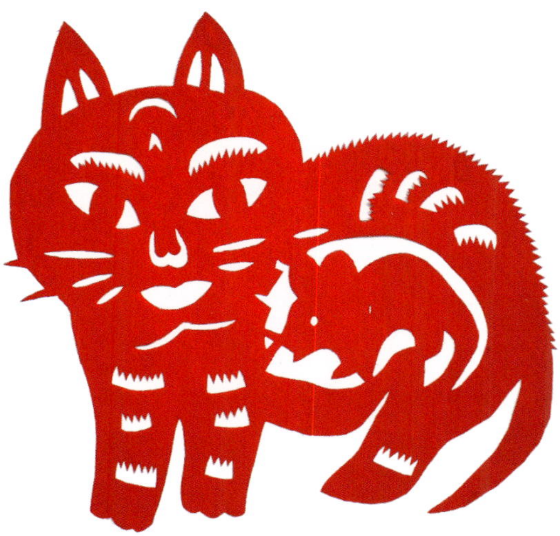

A Little Cat

The little cat is happy enough to have just eaten a mouse.

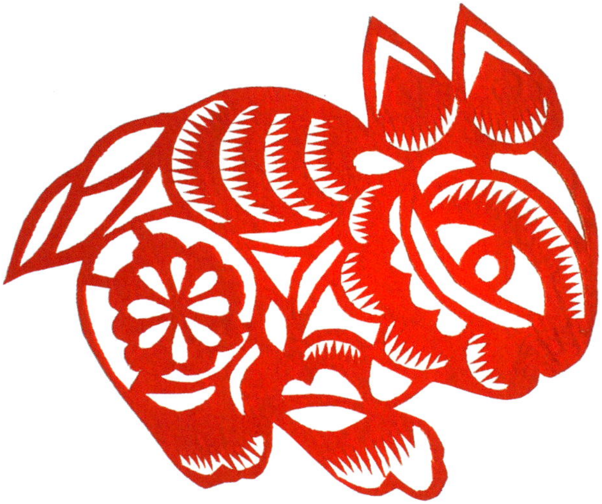

The Domestic Rabbit

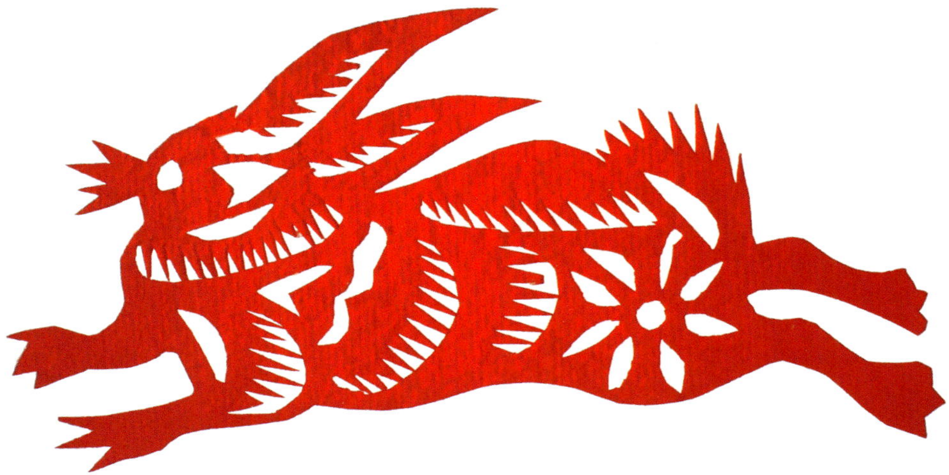

The Wild Rabbit

These two pictures are in the shape of a rabbit. The above is a timid and coy domestic rabbit but the latter is a wild rabbit jumping and running. The difference between the two rabbits in character and expression are all created by a scissors and a piece of paper. What eyes the farming woman has and how powerful her ability for artistic expression is!

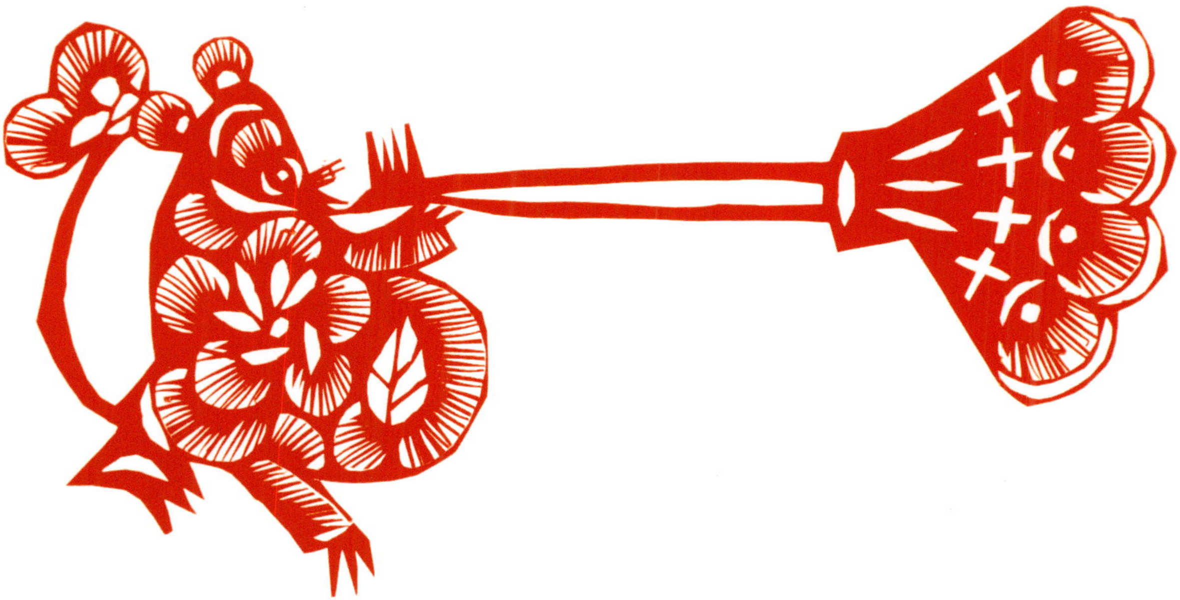

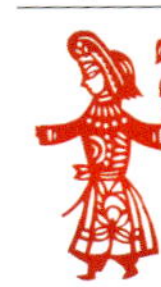

A Mouse Getting Married

A mouse is born to chew furniture and clothes and steal grain, cotton and food. It is really awful that they ruin all the organic matter that people lovingly cherish. However, it is hard to understand why people not only sing for it with compassion but also compose many stories such as the "mouse getting married" and the "mouse marrying off his daughter," which are popular among the people.

The Honour Guard

According to historical documents written during the Qin Dynasty more than 2,200 years ago, the hateful mouse was placed in first position on the list of the twelve symbolic animals. Moreover, it has never been changed through changes of dozens of dynasties. How did this come about?

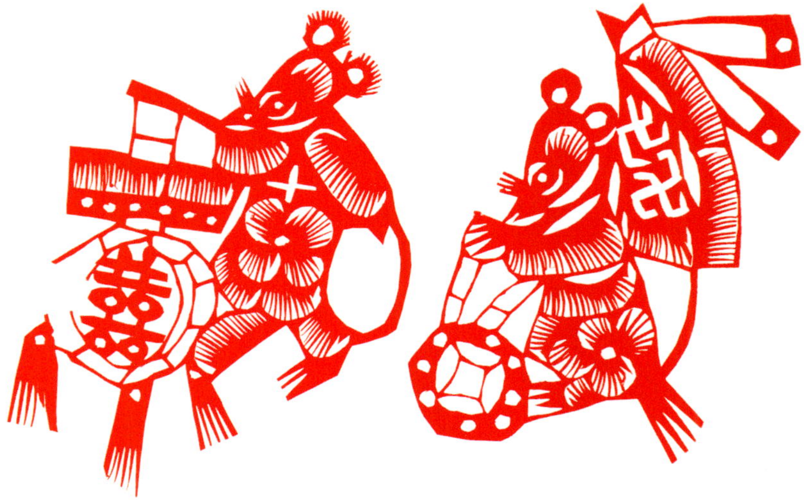

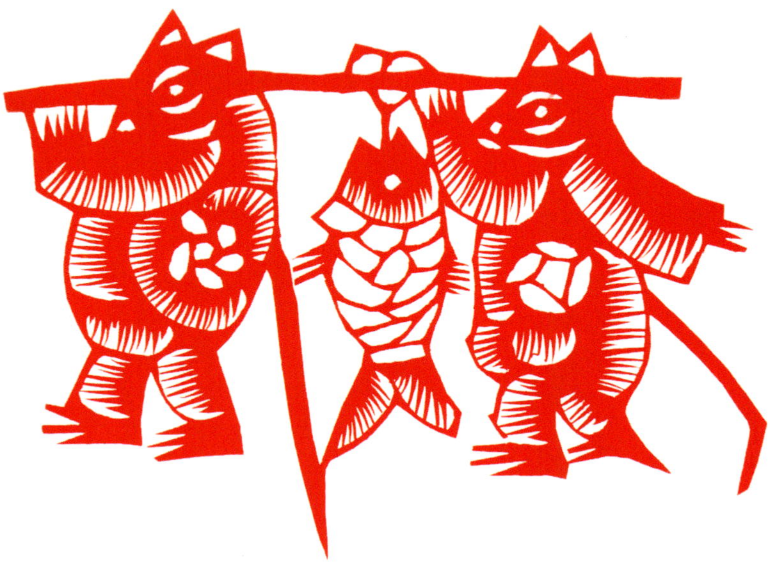

Carrying Carp

With respect to the artistic expression of these paper-cuts there is a common link i.e. the straight lines are not straight and the curved lines are not even. However, due to their proper disposal the lines are harmoniously blended.

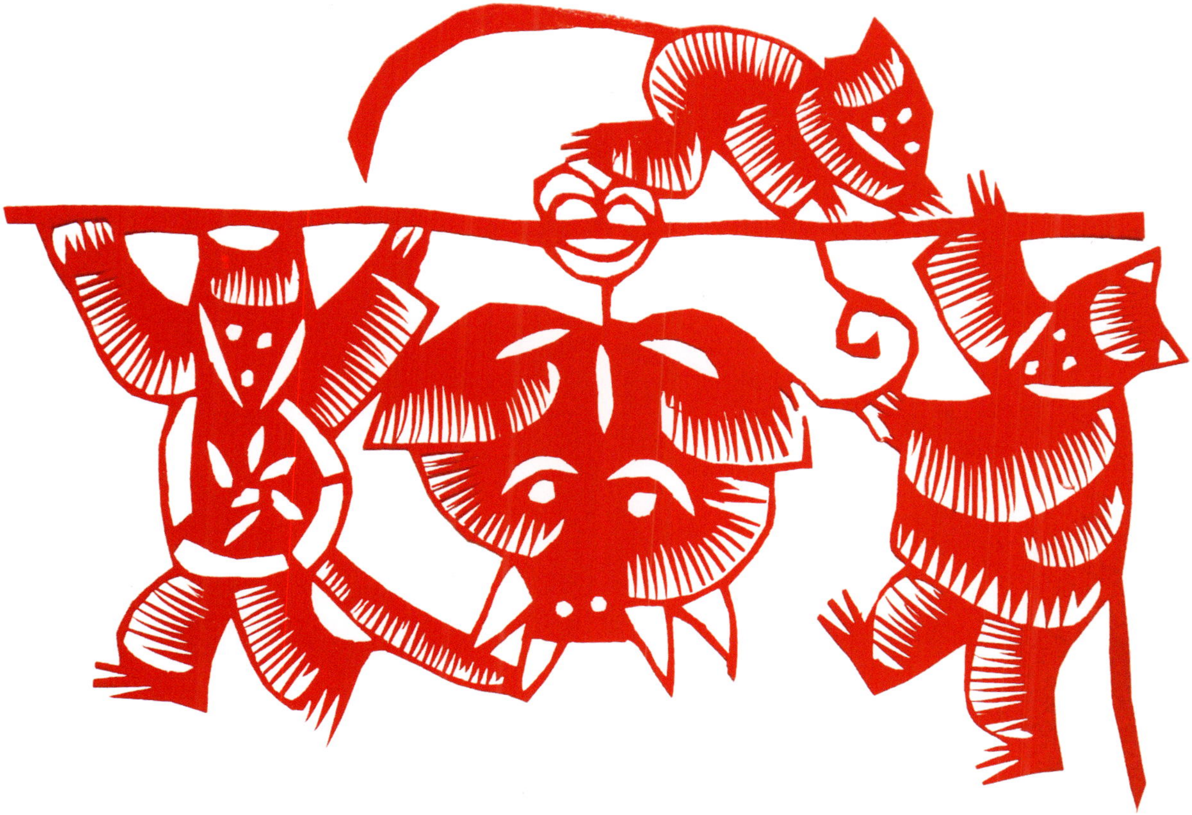

Preparing a Wedding Feast

It impresses people that the straight lines are not rigid and the curves are not gentle. However, they blend together well making the whole picture full of strength.

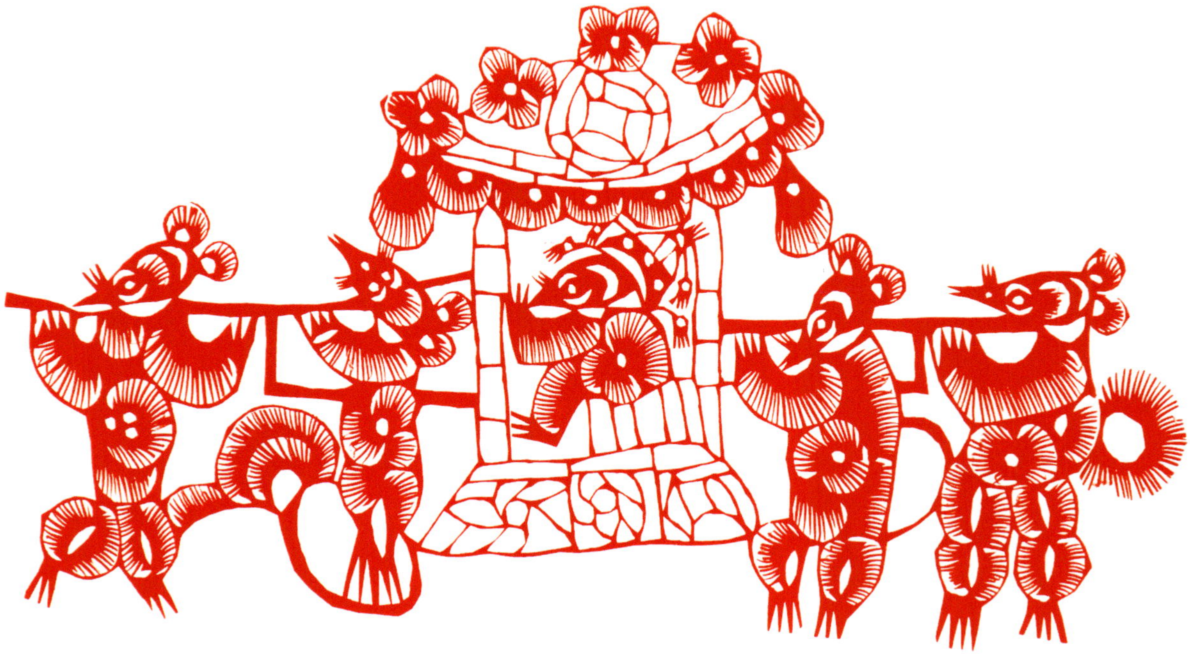

Bride's Sedan Chair

Such a complicated picture is due to the ingenious arrangement of empty space and solid. The thin lines of the sedan set off the solid lines of the flowers on its top and the bride in it.

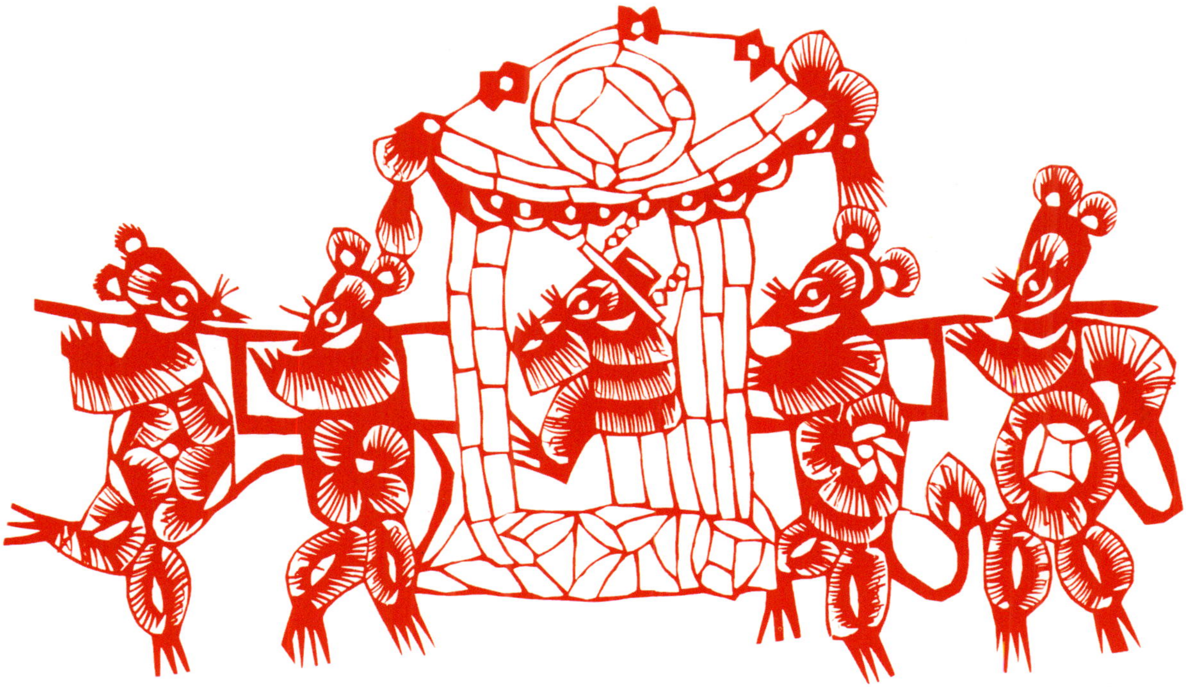

Bride Groom's Sedan Chair

The Chinese paper-cut itself is a demonstration of the old concept of *Yin* and *Yang* which coexist. Therefore, only by hollowing out some parts could the image come out.

Yin and *Yang* coexist and make infinite changes and they combine to multiply lives endlessly.

It is the traditional cultural concept of China.

It is the traditional artistic spirit of China.

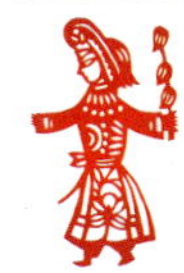

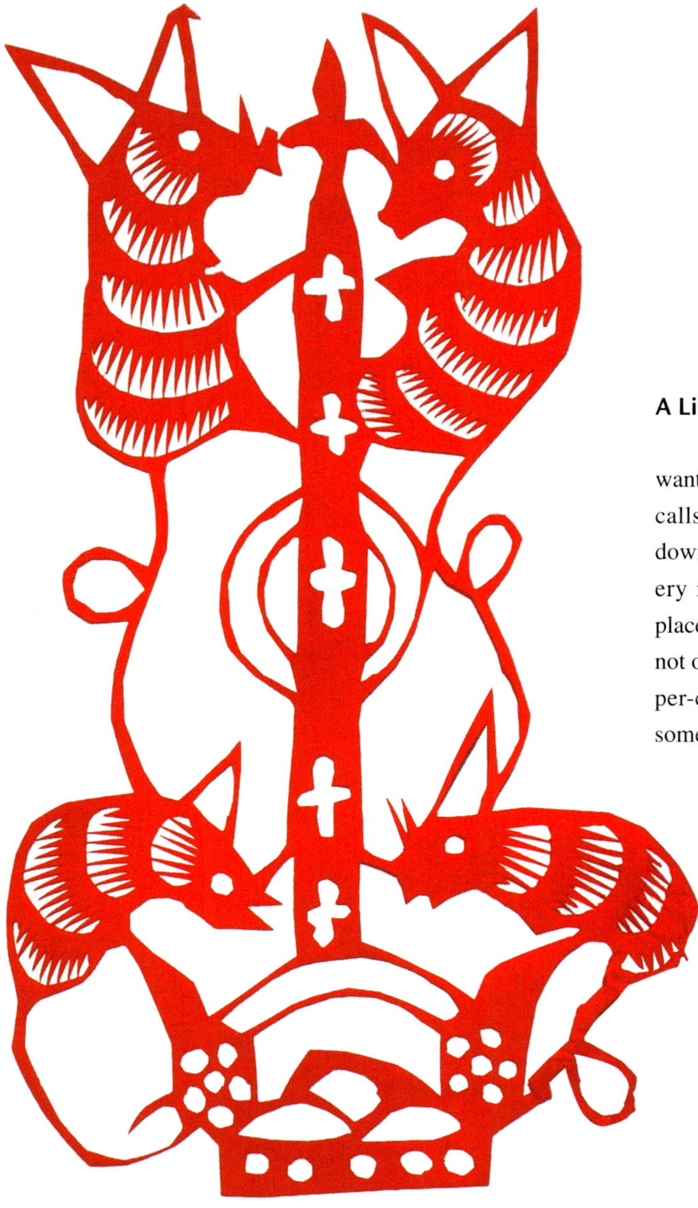

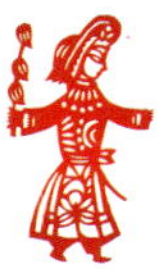

A Little Mouse Goes up the Lamp Stand

"A Little mouse goes up the lamp stand. He wants to steal the oil to eat but can not get down. He calls grandma for help but is refused. So he rolls down like a wheel." Nobody knows when this nursery rhyme spread even to remote and backward places though there was no radio and telephone. It is not only widely sung but also widely depicted in paper-cuts. Even now this rhyme and picture arouse some elders' nostalgia.